KABBALAH

INSPIRATIONS

KABBALAH

INSPIRATIONS

MYSTIC THEMES, TEXTS AND SYMBOLS

JEREMY ROSEN

CHARTWELL
BOOKS, INC.

**To everyone who tries to be a good person
and make the world a better place.**

Kabbalah Inspirations
Jeremy Rosen

Managing Editor: Kirsten Chapman
Managing Designer: Daniel Sturges
Picture Researcher: Julia Ruxton
Commissioned artwork: Sally Taylor (Artist Partners Ltd)

1 3 5 7 9 10 8 6 4 2

This edition published in 2013 by
CHARTWELL BOOKS, INC.
A division of BOOK SALES, INC.
276 Fifth Avenue Suite 206
New York, New York 10001
USA

First published in the UK and Ireland in 2005 by
Duncan Baird Publishers, an imprint of
Watkins Publishing Limited
Sixth Floor, 75 Wells Street,
London W1T 3QH

A member of Osprey Group

A CIP record for this book is available from the British Library

Typeset in Joanna
Color reproduction by Scanhouse, Malaysia
Printed in China by Imago

ISBN: 978-0-7858-2980-5

Notes
The abbreviations ce and bce are used throughout this book:
ce Common Era (the equivalent of ad)
bce Before the Common Era (the equivalent of bc)

"Ten are the numbers of the mystical sefirot,

ten and not nine, ten and not eleven.

Learn this wisdom, and be wise understanding it.

Investigate these numbers, and draw knowledge from them.

Follow the design in its purity,

and you will pass before the Creator seated on His throne."

SEFER YETZIRAH 1.4

CONTENTS

Introduction: Jewish Mysticism

The Hebrew word *kabbalah* simply means "to receive" or "tradition". On a general level it refers to the Jewish mysticism that dates back to the biblical period. In a more technical sense, the Kabbalah is a body of esoteric literature that emerged in medieval Spain and France and looked deeply into biblical texts to discover secrets of how to harness divine energy and establish direct contact with God.

For some Kabbalists communion with the Divine can be achieved through study and thought. Others follow a system of rituals and practices, such as meditation and fasting, that help to detach us from mundane activities and live a spiritual life. All Kabbalists look to language as a means of connecting with God, because, as the book of *Genesis* tells us, God used Hebrew words as the tools of creation (see page 16).

BIBLICAL ORIGINS

The Kabbalah did not spring out of a vacuum. The prophets of the *Bible* – particularly Abraham, Isaac, Jacob and Moses – all offered personal visions of Judaism in which they sought to understand God. Moses asked to see His face. God's reply, that Moses could see only His "back", indicates how difficult it is

> "And God said to Moses, 'You cannot see my face. No living being can see my face and live.' And God said, 'Here is a place very close to me, and you will stand on this rock. And when my glory passes by I will hide you in a crack in the rock and place my hand over you until I have passed and then I will remove my hand and you will see my back, but you will not see my face.'"

EXODUS 33.24

for mortals to acquire this understanding. We can see divine actions, but a complete vision of God may not be possible until we reach the spiritual world.

In 586 BCE the Babylonians forced the Jews out of Israel, destroying the Temple built by Solomon to house the Ark of the Covenant. But this displacement led to a new era of Jewish creativity. While in exile the prophet Ezekiel had a dramatic vision of a chariot that would inspire later mystics. When the Jews returned to Israel in 538 BCE, formal religion was re-established, but it coexisted with new, less structured forms of worship and study. Various sects emerged. There were ideological conflicts between the established priesthood and revolutionary rabbinic academies. The period either side of the Common Era was one of turbulence, but it was also rich in alternative theologies and mysticism.

The *Torah* and the *Talmud*

The two primary sources for the Jewish religious tradition are the *Torah* and the *Talmud*. The word *Torah* originally referred to the first five books of the *Bible*, which are also known as *The Five Books of Moses* or *The Pentateuch*. These books are regarded as the essential revelation that was given to Moses on Mount Sinai. However, in time *Torah* came to be used as a general term to describe both the ethical and ritual laws that were contained in these five books and the Jewish way of life that was committed to these laws.

The original revelation contained in the *Torah* is called the "Written Law". Over the succeeding generations this law was expanded and interpreted, to produce a tradition of "Oral Law". Eventually these oral traditions and laws were written down to become the *Talmud*.

The *Talmud* is the most important and authoritative document in Judaism after the *Bible*. The text consists of two main parts: the *Mishnah*, compiled by Rabbi Judah the Prince in Israel around 200 CE; and the *Gemara*, which comprises discussion and commentaries on the *Mishnah*, completed around 500 CE.

There are actually two versions of the *Talmud*: the Jerusalem *Talmud* and the later Babylonian *Talmud*, which are named for where they were written. The Babylonian *Talmud* is more substantial, and is what most people mean when they refer to the *Talmud*.

THE TALMUDIC ERA

The ideas and culture of the first 1,000 years of post-biblical Judaism were compiled in the *Talmud* (see box, opposite). Most rabbis of this period were concerned with preserving mainstream religion, but they also looked in the *Torah* for ideas that were *nistar* (hidden) – a term that also refers to the "hidden aspect of God". The *Talmud* mentioned *ma'aseh mercava* (secrets of the chariot) and *ma'aseh bereishit* (secrets of creation), both of which were esoteric subjects, to be studied only by scholars.

The *Talmud* also contains folklore, astrology and tales of miracle workers, many of which would later find their way into the mystical tradition. But by far the most important character of the *Talmud* is Rabbi Shimon Ben Yochai, who became the personification of profound mysticism (see page 33). A central work of the Kabbalah, the *Zohar* (*Brightness*), was later attributed to him.

THE BOOK OF CREATION

In 70 CE the Romans seized Jerusalem and destroyed the Second Temple. Although the Jewish people eventually managed to recapture the city, life here went into moral decline. Small groups of scholars and devotees set up sects around the Dead Sea, where they continued the mystical traditions. Out of these groups emerged the *Sefer Yetzirah* (*Book of Creation*), the first text to describe kabbalistic ideas. It clearly states that there is an alternative way of looking at the world.

THE MIDDLE AGES

Around the 12th and 13th centuries, Europe was in religious upheaval and Jewish people were suffering persecution at the hands of the Christians. This fostered a period of Jewish creativity. The *Hasidei Ashkenaz* (Pious Men of Germany) introduced customs and practices aimed at heightening spirituality, ecstasy and piety. A new type of mysticism grew and spread.

The more the Christian world used philosophical tools to try to prove its supremacy, the more the Jewish people retreated into mysticism to reassure themselves of their spiritual heritage. In the 13th century the alternative philosophy of the *Hasidei Ashkenaz* took root among scholars in southern France and northern Spain. From these groups there emerged new mystical works in Aramaic, such as the *Bahir* (*Book of Light*) and the *Zohar* (*Brightness*). The latter – a collection of monologues and commentaries on the *Torah* – was to become the most widespread book of the Kabbalah.

As life under the Spanish Christian monarchs became unstable, the non-rational world offered an escape and a comfort. Some mystics such as Abraham Abulafia courted danger by preaching messianism – the idea that a saviour, a descendant of King David, would gather the Jews in Jerusalem and initiate an earthly reign of peace and harmony.

THE MIDDLE EAST

The Jews were expelled from Spain in 1492. This led to a movement of great Jewish thinkers and mystics to Italy, from Italy to Greece and Turkey, and from there to the newly established "city of refuge" in Safed in Galilee.

Safed became a dynamic centre for a wave of kabbalistic innovation. Figures such as Moses Cordovero, Isaac Luria and Chaim Vital refined and combined earlier kabbalistic ideas with new ecstatic practices. They popularized the Kabbalah as a way of reaching God and living a fuller, more spiritual life. Elevating experience over scholarship, they encouraged a wider, nonacademic audience to join them.

However, it was not long before the Kabbalah was also adopted by magical and superstitious fringe movements. The excesses of some of these sects and their false messiahs, such as Shabbetai Zevi and Jacob Frank, led to a campaign to expunge mysticism from Jewish life.

"A woman has a mystical capacity to open up and reveal the hidden soul
of a man. Through her spirit she can bring to the soul of a man a deeper
dimension of suffering and joy that opens up the wellsprings of his inner
being … . When such a Woman of Valour is not there, then the spirit
of mysticism must work in her stead to achieve the same goal."

ABRAHAM ISAAC KOOK (1865–1935), OLAT REIYAH 1.62

With the advent of the Enlightenment, the Kabbalah became more marginalized, particularly in Western Europe.

18TH-CENTURY REVIVAL

In the 18th century the Kabbalah experienced a dramatic revival with the development of Hasidism in Eastern Europe. This movement, led by a figure known as the Baal Shem Tov, took Luria's ideas, popularized them and, to some extent, legitimized the kabbalistic approach to life. Early hasidic masters were suffused with the free, experimental mood of Safed mysticism. However, like many revolutionary movements, Hasidism soon lost its innovative, anti-establishment character and became part of the structured orthodoxy.

Nevertheless, small groups of learned men – and occasionally women – continued to keep mysticism alive through their writings and private esoteric practices. They came to dominate Jewish life among the poorer and less educated communities. In the North African countries particularly, kabbalistic practices were associated with folk medicine and "wonder rabbis". Here the Kabbalah became more of a tool of popular superstition than genuine spiritual elevation.

THE KABBALAH TODAY

Over time the *Zohar* has come to acquire a canonical status on a par with talmudic literature. Although many kabbalistic practices and meditations have been forgotten or ignored by all but a few, the influence of the Kabbalah on Jewish practical and liturgical life is profound.

Why has the Kabbalah become so fashionable now? In the West many people have begun to react against purely rational and scientific thought. For although technology has advanced, it has not helped us to deal with moral and spiritual issues. Thus many now turn to alternative ways of coping with life and its pressures. Established Western religions have lost many followers as people become more individualistic and experimental. But charismatic alternatives and Eastern traditions have flourished.

And so it is with the Kabbalah. Its long association with rebellion against authority attracts those who have been alienated by formal, structured religions. Others are inspired by the amazing similarities between the Kabbalah and Eastern systems of self-realization and healing. And still, in its authentic form, the Kabbalah offers a mysticism that can help people to bring spirituality into their everyday lives.

The Hebrew Alphabet

There are 22 letters in the Hebrew alphabet, each of which also has a numerical value. To the mystics letters were the tools of creation, and meditating on them can help us to commune with God.

The Hebrew language functions on several levels. Some letters are made up of others: *Aleph*, for example, comprises a diagonal *Vav* with a *Yod* either side. It can lead us to think of God, whose name is made up of *Yod*, *Hey* and *Vav*. Words can also tell stories: *AMT* means "truth" but also includes the first, middle and last letters of the alphabet, conveying the idea that "truth is all-encompassing".

Mystics are also interested in types of Hebrew letters, particularly: singles, which have one sound; and doubles, which can be hard or soft depending on context. Kabbalists see the stable singles as the building blocks of creation, while doubles reflect the male and female aspects of God. The Kabbalah adds a further category: mother letters, which represent the elements of creation.

LETTER	NAME	TRANSLITERATION	NUMBER	TYPE
א	Aleph	A/E/I	1	mother
ב	Bet	B	2	double
ג	Gimmel	G	3	double
ד	Daled	D	4	double
ה	Hey	H	5	single
ו	Vav	V	6	single
ז	Zayin	Z	7	single
ח	Chet	Ch	8	single
ט	Tet	T	9	single
י	Yod	Y	10	single
כ	Chaf	C	20	double
ל	Lamed	L	30	single
מ	Mem	M	40	mother
נ	Nun	N	50	single
ס	Samekh	S	60	single
ע	Ayin	A/E/I	70	single
פ	Peh	P	80	double
צ	Tsadi	Ts	90	single
ק	Kuf	K	100	single
ר	Reysh	R	200	double
ש	Shin	Sh	300	mother
ת	Tav	T	400	double

CHAPTER ONE

ENCOUNTERS WITH GOD

Judaism has always been a religion of form
and structure. It has also been a religion of
charismatic teachers and mystics. They laid the
foundations for a "hidden" way of communing
directly with God that would develop into a
complex mystical system known as the Kabbalah.

The Founding Fathers

The biblical "fathers" of the Kabbalah – Abraham, Isaac, Jacob and Moses – are quite different in character. This led to the idea that they worshipped and experienced God in personal ways.

ABRAHAM AND ISAAC

According to the *Bible*, Abraham was the founder of the monotheistic religion. He was born into a time of idol worship, but came to recognize that there was a single creative force behind the universe. He dedicated his life to teaching others how to experience God.

A 13th-century Pentateuch illustration of an angel preventing Abraham from sacrificing his son Isaac.

Abraham was sufficiently at ease with his Maker to be able to argue with Him over the destruction of Sodom and Gomorrah. He showed that it was possible to engage and struggle with God.

Despite this closeness to the Divine, however, Abraham's life was neither easy nor secure. He was subjected to tests of his faith, starting with God's request that he leave his home and seek a distant country. Faith is not an answer, nor a solution: it is a voyage of exploration.

The crucial event in Abraham's life was when God commanded him to sacrifice his son Isaac. This makes us question Abraham's relationship with God. Did God really tell him to kill his son? Could Abraham have misunderstood?

These and other problems occupied later Jewish mystics. Was it possible to re-create the type of communication that existed between God and Abraham? How did Abraham reach God? What were his "special tools, crystals and secrets", as they were later referred to in the *Sefer Yetzirah* (Book of Creation)?

Isaac's role here is also significant. He totally accepted that it was his fate to be sacrificed. He is the passive mystic, who later "went out to meditate in the fields toward evening time" and so was credited with inventing meditation.

JACOB

Genesis tells how Isaac married Rebecca and had twin sons, Jacob and Esau. When Rebecca tricked the elderly Isaac into giving Jacob a blessing meant for Esau, Esau became so angry that Jacob was forced to flee for his life. On the journey he had a dream of angels on a ladder (see quotation, page 22) in

> "And Jacob left Beer Sheva and went toward Haran. And he reached the place where he would spend the night, and as the sun set he took some stones and rested his head. And he dreamed that a ladder was placed on the ground and it reached up to heaven and angels of God were moving up and down on it."
>
> **GENESIS 28.10**

which the voice of God told him that he and his descendants would be blessed.

After many years Jacob sought reconciliation with Esau and travelled back to his homeland. Alone at night he met a "man" who engaged him in a fight. At dawn his assailant tried to get away, but Jacob would not let go until the "man" blessed him. Jacob had realized that this figure was actually an angel. The angel renamed him Israel, meaning "to struggle with Man and God and to survive".

This narrative is crucial to mysticism. It illustrates that belief in God requires a struggle. This struggle is ongoing and involves the body as well as the mind and soul. Jacob had been close to God prior to this encounter, but he did not live in certainty and peace. Nor was he protected from the dangers of the material world. If we want to be close to God, we cannot withdraw from this world: we have to engage with it, both physically and mentally.

MOSES

In mainstream Judaism Moses is the law-giver, but in the mystical tradition he is the teacher of secrets. He holds a unique position in the *Bible* as the vehicle of divine revelation: God speaks to him "face to face" and "mouth to mouth".

There are seven different names for God in the *Bible*, each denoting a different facet of divinity and a different way in which God relates to humanity. Names are important as symbols, not of the outer being but of the essence of a person and, indeed, of God.

When Moses asked to "see God's face", God replied that no human can see God and live. Moses was shown only His "back". When Moses asked for God's "essential" name, God replied, "*I am that I am.*" If Moses could understand this answer, which is God's name, he would be able to understand the nature of God.

The location of Moses' grave was kept secret so that people would not be tempted to follow and worship him instead of the *Torah* and God.

Moses met God at the burning bush on Mount Horeb. Fire symbolizes God's interaction with humans on a mystical level.

Elijah

O ne of the most popular figures in the Jewish tradition, Elijah was a champion of the poor and oppressed, as well as a mystic whose use of fire is a metaphor for his sacred powers.

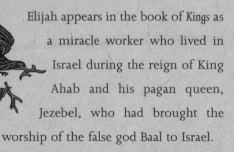

Elijah appears in the book of *Kings* as a miracle worker who lived in Israel during the reign of King Ahab and his pagan queen, Jezebel, who had brought the worship of the false god Baal to Israel.

Elijah challenged the queen's prophets to a trial to determine whether God or Baal was the true deity. On Mount Carmel both sides offered sacrifices. Elijah prayed to God, and fire came down from heaven to ignite his sacrifice. The supporters of Baal were defeated.

When Elijah died, a "chariot of fire" appeared and "a whirlwind" took him up to Heaven – images that would later play an essential role in expressing mystical ideas. Elijah continues to appear throughout the *Talmud* and the Kabbalah as God's representative on Earth. It is said in the *Talmud* that, after he has settled any unresolved theological disputes, he will announce the arrival of the Messiah.

Opposite: Elijah's victory forced him to flee to a desert cave, where he was fed by ravens.

Ezekiel and Daniel

W hen the Babylonians forced the Jewish people out of Israel in 586 BCE, the exiles came into contact with other ideas about the nature of God, life after death and the prophesied End of Days. These ideas formed the nucleus of new mystical traditions.

Physical displacement was not the only effect of exile. The Babylonians destroyed the magnificent Temple built by Solomon to house the Ark of the Covenant. The Temple had been the primary place of communion between the Jewish people and God. The spiritual loss was profound.

Written in exile in Babylon, the prophet Ezekiel's message to the Jewish people was not to abandon hope: he reassured them that they would return to Israel. Just as Moses had had a vision of God at the burning bush as an augury of his leading the Israelite slaves out of Egypt, so Ezekiel experienced a dramatic divine vision in Babylon.

The first chapter of Ezekiel contains a powerful, impressionistic description of this vision. It was an intricate composite of images, human, animal and bird, surrounded by ice, lightning and the elements of air, fire and water – of which fire predominated. The vision rose,

Daniel

Also writing in Babylon was the prophet Daniel. His use of Aramaic as well as Hebrew indicates the impact of exile on Jewish life – a significant cultural shift. But Daniel also introduced the idea of the End of Days. In the book that bears his name, it is obvious that he intended this vision to refer to an imminent return from exile to the Land of Israel – resurrection in a national sense. However, in the following generations Daniel's vision became the basis of apocalyptic hopes for the end of the world, universal resurrection and a new, redemptive way of living.

revolved and moved on whirling disks within disks against a background of throbbing, flashing lights and sounds. Eventually Ezekiel saw a throne of sapphire with a human figure sitting on it, and a disembodied voice spoke to him.

Although some aspects of Ezekiel's vision, such as the human and animal figures, were familiar, the overall effect was almost beyond imagination. The wonderful language he used became a lexicon of terms for later mystics. Ezekiel portrayed the heavenly fire using words such as *bezek* (lightning) and *chashmal* (which has come to mean "electricity"), and he introduced the idea of *ratsui ve shuv*, a magnetic attraction and repulsion built into our relationship with God.

The End of Days

The Babylonian Empire was destroyed by the Persians in 538 BCE and the Jews were able to return to Israel. Religious life was reconstructed; new forms of leadership and different sects emerged. Many were waiting for salvation, the End of Days and a new world order.

The Persian Empire fell in turn to Alexander the Great. Alexander's empire broke up with his death in 323 BCE. This led to a surge in Jewish spiritual creativity. Apocalyptic books sought solutions to the political and religious upheavals.

These books shared certain common themes. The world would descend into chaos. There would be battles between the forces of good and evil. A messiah figure would emerge from the desert to transform humanity. Those who had prepared themselves through religious discipline and correct behaviour would survive to enjoy a new world suffused with the spirit of God.

The later book of *Enoch* is named after the biblical character whom God had taken from Earth to a higher level of spirituality. Parts of the book deal with celestial cycles and levels. Others introduce disciplines that were designed to enhance spirituality and open up believers to the experience of God.

Heavenly Palaces
and Divine Humans

Two kinds of mystical writings started to appear around 2,000 years ago: *hekhalot* literature, which was concerned with the "palaces of Heaven"; and *shiur koma*, which considered the essence of Man and his relationship with the God, in whose image he was made.

In the Maccabean revolt of 167 BCE, Jews rose up against the Greeks and recaptured Jerusalem. However, the ruling dynasty they established soon fell into moral decline. Many faithful Jews withdrew from society and established sects around the Dead Sea. Here they created an influential mystical literature.

Around this time many scholars were studying astronomy and astrology. The Dead Sea sects picked up on this interest,

and they wrote literature suggesting that if we could understand the stars and the planets – the *hekhalot* (heavenly halls) in which God resided – we could draw closer to God and discover how to use His powers to transform life on Earth.

Shiur koma literature, which also emerged from these sects, was concerned with the measure of Man. If Man was made in the image of God, then a better understanding of how humans work might lead to a clearer under-standing of God's nature.

Jews seeking to study these areas were expected to be already leading a reli-gious life and following the *Torah*. However, some scholars wanted to achieve a higher level of spirituality, and so started delving deeper into the secrets of Heaven and Earth.

CHARIOTS AND CREATION

The *Talmud* – comprising the *Mishnah* (compiled *c.*200 CE) and the *Gemara* (compiled *c.*500 CE) – records the ideas of Judaism in the 1,000 years after the

The seven heavenly halls of hekhalot liter-ature are guarded by angels, who admit only those who know the secret formulae.

biblical period. It discusses two mystical themes: ma'aseh mercava and ma'aseh bereishit. Both were a conscious antidote to the prevailing Greek rationalism, which implied that human reason was superior to divine intervention.

Ma'aseh mercava (secrets of the chariot) explored the nature of God. Speculation centred around Ezekiel's description of the divine chariot (see quotation, opposite). The biblical text was said to contain secrets, which once understood could give the power to create life and perform miracles.

Ma'aseh bereishit (secrets of creation) sought to understand the nature of the universe, and speculation often

An illustration from a commentary on the book of Job (c.945 CE) showing Ezekiel's vision of the chariot.

> "And I looked and I saw a whirlwind coming from the north, there was
> heavy cloud and fire glowing and an aura around and from inside flashed
> bolts of fire. And from within appeared four spirits. ... They had the overall
> shape of humans. But each had four faces and four wings. ... and they were
> moving as the spirit drew them. And out of the aura came lightning."
>
> **EZEKIEL 1.4**

focused on *Genesis* and its hidden meanings. The most important text of this tradition was the *Sefer Yetzirah*, dating from around 200 CE or later (see page 36).

The *Talmud* contains many stories of miracle workers, popular teachers and mystics. But the personality who stands out as a champion of *ma'aseh mercava* and *ma'aseh bereishit* is Rabbi Shimon Ben (or Bar in Aramaic) Yochai. He was not only a profound mystic but also a determined teacher, despite Roman laws against the dissemination of what was considered "subversive thinking".

Shimon's challenge to the authorities meant that, like Elijah, he and his son were forced to hide in a cave for many years. Here they attained such high levels of enlightenment that they found it difficult to readjust to the mundane standards of their contemporaries after they ended their confinement.

CHAPTER TWO

THE EMERGENCE OF THE KABBALAH

What is now known as the Kabbalah is a body
of literature and ideology that grew out of
Provence and Catalonia 1,000 years ago.
But it could not have come about without – nor
can it be understood independently of – earlier
mystical ideas and religious sources.

The Sefer Yetzirah

T he *Sefer Yetzirah* (Book of Creation) is the most important text of the early Kabbalah, containing the movement's basic mystical ideas and concepts, including the idea of the *sefirot*.

In the *Talmud* there is a reference to a "Book of Creation" that contains the secrets of how to form life. This reference may have been the inspiration for the *Sefer Yetzirah*.

The exact date and authorship of the *Sefer Yetzirah* are unknown, but the book uses terms that are post-talmudic, which suggests that it dates from 200 CE or later. It is written in a poetic style, and states in its last chapter that an angel visited Abraham and gave him the secrets of the universe contained in the book.

By the end of the first millennium, the *Sefer Yetzirah* was the most read, annotated and commented on mystical text.

WORDS AND NUMBERS

According to its opening chapter, the world has to be understood on three levels: the written, the spoken and the numerical – in Hebrew these words share the same linguistic root, SPR. These levels provide different but interrelated ways of describing and understanding the spiritual and physical worlds.

The "written" refers to Hebrew text, the vehicle used to reveal the *Torah*. In addition each Hebrew letter has a numerical value (see page 17). So every word can be seen as letters, heard through sounds and thought of in numbers. The main names of God, for example, revolve around the letters *Yod* and *Hey*, the numbers five and ten respectively. But there are secret ways of pronouncing these names of God.

In the early chapters of *Genesis*, when God commands the creation of the world, the expression "Let there be …" is repeated ten times. So "ten" was taken to be a crucial clue to understanding how God created the world.

An angelic messenger revealed to Abraham the secrets of creation, which are contained in the Sefer Yetzirah.

THE SEFIROT

The *Sefer Yetzirah* is the first text to contain a systematic description of the *sefirot*, which are central to kabbalistic thought. If God is nonphysical, how does He interact with the physical world? The *Talmud* suggested the idea of *Schechina*, God's presence on Earth. The *Sefer Yetzirah* describes how the infinite and nonphysical God, *Ein Sof*, is interconnected with *Schechina* through the *sefirot*.

Just as humans have different facets and characteristics, so symbolically does God. The *sefirot* (singular: *sefira*) are the ten categories that represent Him. In the *Sefer Yetzirah* they are multidimensional energy sources. They are described as *blima*, which means "amazing" as well as "nonexistent" or "without substance".

The *sefirot* are linked through letters of the Hebrew alphabet. There are three types of letters: mothers, doubles, and singles (see page 16). Each type has power and a function in communication and creation. The three mother letters (*Aleph*, *Mem* and *Shin*) have a stabilizing role and symbolize the primordial elements of all living things. The seven doubles represent the ambiguity of elements and changeable attitudes. The 12 remaining singles are the stable building blocks of the universe.

The *Sefer Yetzirah* shows how letters and the *sefirot* connect everything in the cosmos. The book draws on astronomy and angelology and links each of the *sefirot* and their letters to celestial bodies, angels, the calendar, the human body and every single act and thought. Earth mirrors Heaven, and thus God enters into everything, including intellectual, emotional and even sexual experience.

Meditation on the Three Mothers

The mother letters function like the scales of justice. *Aleph* is the fulcrum and air passing in and out of the body. Balance good and evil through deep breathing and meditation.

Aleph is air, it travels up and down the centre of the body.

Mem is good and *Shin* is evil.

Mem is the right hand and *Shin* is the left.

Hold the palms out,

Mem is the right and *Shin* is the left.

Breathe in and out.

Balance the power of evil against the power of good.

Five *sefirot* on the right.

Five *sefirot* on the left.

Breathe in and out.

Cleanse the body, clear the mind

And fly to Heaven.

From the Sefer Yetzirah 2.1 and 3.1

Meditation on the Six Directions

Movement helps us to feel the auras of divine energy. Perform this while standing facing Jerusalem (assumed here to be in the East). See page 60 for the names of the *sefirot*.

ROM (upward): Raise your arms above your head with your palms facing a handspan apart. Reach beyond the universe to *Ein Sof*. Bring your arms back down. Repeat for each name of the *sefirot*.

TACHAT (downward): Bend at your waist and lower your hands, a handspan apart, to touch the Earth. Feel the Earth and the world of the *Schechina*. Stand up again. Repeat for each name of the *sefirot*.

MIZRACH (eastward): Place your hands on your waist and bow forward as low as possible. Stand up again. Repeat for each name of the *sefirot*.

MAARAV (westward): Place your hands on your waist and lean your torso as far back as possible. Stand up again. Repeat for each name of the *sefirot*.

DAROM (southward): Place your hands on your waist and twist to the right. Return to face the front again. Repeat for each name of the *sefirot*.

TSAFON (northward): Place your hands on your waist and twist to the left. Return to face the front again. Repeat for each name of the *sefirot*.

By Abulafia, based on the Sefer Yetzirah 1.13

The Pious Men of Germany

In the Rhineland in the 12th and 13th centuries, a group of mystics developed a highly ascetic variation of Judaism. They became known as the *Hasidei Ashkenaz* (Pious Men of Germany).

The Middle Ages saw the persecution of Jewish people in several Western European countries and the expulsion of Jews from others. In northern Germany this led to the emergence of the *Hasidei Ashkenaz*, a movement that placed emphasis on accepting suffering stoically and on self-denial and martyrdom as a reaction against the harshness of life on Earth. Several communities chose to commit suicide rather than submit to forced conversion or death.

Such convictions had been influenced by texts like the 11th-century *Chovot HaLevavot* (*Duties of the Heart*) by Bahya Ibn Pakuda, which talks about self-discipline in pursuit of the Divine. The *Hasidei Ashkenaz* based their thinking on this concern with ethics and the obligations of the heart and mind.

The *Sefer Hasidim* (*Book of the Pious*), by Judah Ben Samuel (1150–1217), was not a book of mystical theory as such, but it placed tremendous emphasis on

piety and holy behaviour as a means of achieving enlightenment and closeness to God. The book stressed that contemplation – described by the term *devekut* (attachment to good) – could lead to direct spiritual communion.

These early Hasidim looked to the End of Days and divine intervention through the Messiah to end their suffering. These ideas were combined with strict self-discipline and self-denial,

Jewish people in 12th- and 13th-century northern Germany were required to wear identifying garments such as conical hats.

leading to a heightened religious atmosphere. Although the *Hasidei Ashkenaz* did not create a major body of mystical theory, they found new ways of understanding traditional sources and laid the foundations for practical Kabbalah through exercises and devotions.

The Bahir

The *Bahir* (*Book of Light*) is another early influential text of the Kabbalah. It is very different in structure from the *Sefer Yetzirah* but shares the same mystical premises.

Although written in a talmudic style and attributed to the first-century Rabbi Nechunia Ben HaKna, the *Bahir* first appeared after the *Sefer Yetzirah*, in the 12th century. It is less systematic than the earlier text, structured as a compilation of mini lectures in which pupils ask their rabbi to help them by explaining difficult concepts, mainly to do with creation but also concerning good and evil.

The *Bahir* shows the influence of gnosticism, the belief that two powers control the universe – a benevolent God constantly challenged by an evil force. Judaism has always rejected the idea that anything could challenge God. But in trying to answer the problem of evil, some early Jewish thinkers reinterpreted gnosticism, explaining that negative forces act only as agents of the Divine, not in competition. In the *Bahir* the idea of *sefirot* was modified to incorporate these negative energies: it was understood that the quality represented by each *sefira* could be both negative and positive at the same time.

"Rabbi Rachumai said, 'Light came before the universe ... .' His pupils said to him, 'But can it make sense to say that before you create Israel you first create a crown for it?' He said, 'That is correct. But I will explain it. Imagine a king who passionately wants to have a son and he discovers a beautiful crown that everyone says is to be magnificent ... . And he said, "I will keep this for my son." They said, "But how do you know your son will be worthy of this?" He said, "Enough! This is the way I have designed my universe to be.""'

BAHIR 1.16

Another key idea of the *Bahir* was that if God is *ayin* (without substance), then humans need to make themselves *ayin* to get closer to God. The book uses biblical references to "sending away" to convey the idea that we need to escape the physical to reach truth. This can be achieved only by disciplining ourselves – through fasting, prayer and meditation.

The *Bahir* was the first Jewish text to talk specifically about the transmigration of souls – the idea that souls are "recycled". This was another way of explaining human suffering. If what happens on Earth is the result of earlier experiences of the soul, then we should not expect to find answers based only on the evidence of the present.

Provence and Northern Spain

During the 12th century southern France and northern Spain were the settings for a conscious attempt to create a body of thought and practice that later came to be known as the Kabbalah.

The most famous of the Provençal rabbis was Isaac the Blind (c.1160–1236). Isaac meditated by imagining the energy of the *sefirot* descending from God and permeating the mind and body. It is Isaac who is credited with giving the *sefirot* the names that are commonly used today.

Isaac divided the Kabbalah into two categories: the theoretical, which tried to find a nonrational way to see the world; and the practical, a way to experience God through exercises and contemplation. This was in direct conflict with established Jewish thought, which opposed diverting energy from *Torah* study and ritual practice.

GERONA AND NACHMANIDES

Isaac's views found a ready audience in northern Spain, particularly Gerona. The Jewish communities here had become a centre of scholarship, but were divided between rationalists and mystics. The rationalists followed the teachings of Maimonides, a legislator and thinker who had written *The Guide to the Perplexed*, a reconciliation of Judaism and philosophy. In contrast, the mystic Moses Ben Nahman (Nachmanides) (1194–1270) argued that religion based on philosophy was arid and doomed to failure.

Nachmanides avoided the extreme complexities of the Kabbalah. He wrote commentaries on the *Bible* and on Maimonides and added mystical dimensions to earlier discourses on the texts. But more importantly he developed the idea that God's presence on Earth could only be experienced through a people, rather than by individuals alone, and that the Land of Israel exercised a unique spiritual energy. Although mysticism was still regarded as esoteric, it flourished under the influence of Nachmanides.

An early kabbalistic text from northern Spain, decorated with the emblems of Castile and León.

Abraham Abulafia

The writings of this charismatic mystic have been highly influential in the Kabbalah. He was the first to introduce physical exercises akin to yoga and he detailed meditational methods as aids to spiritual enlightenment. Some even considered him the Messiah.

Abraham Abulafia (1240–c.1291) was a scholar who was born in Spain but travelled in Italy, Sicily, Greece and Israel. One of his most important texts was *Ohr HaSechel* (*Light of Intellect*), in which he argued that rational intellectualism was just the first stage in enlightenment and that we have to involve the whole body in mystical exercises if we want fully to

A 14th-century Passover Haggadah. The crucial word, "to cry out", is emphasized.

Morning Meditation

We need to prepare before prayer. First we purify ourselves physically through washing. Then we must remove all mundane thoughts. See page 60 for the names of the *sefirot*.

Before morning prayers sit on a chair or on the floor with a straight back. Clear your mind. Close your eyes and let your eyes stare at the backs of your lids. You will see white and black clouds, patterns or flashes like the chaos of creation. Imagine cleansing your mind and your body.

Breathe in deeply from the bottom of your stomach counting five, and out slowly counting five. Ten divine breaths enter your body.

Repeat the series of ten breaths, thinking the name of each *sefira* as you breathe.

Apply each *sefira* to yourself one by one. "Turn it over and over." Start with *Keter* at your head and work down to *Schechina* at your feet.

Repeat this exercise in the afternoon before the *Mincha* prayer. Consider how you are acting on the issues of the day so far. Which *sefira* or *sefirot* need to be emphasized or minimized?

Repeat this exercise in the evening before the *Maariv* prayer. Which *sefirot* have you used well this past day and which have you not?

By Abulafia, based on the Sefer Yetzirah 2.1

The Five Movements of Transformation

There is physical creativity and spiritual creativity. By making these movements in the physical world, we reinforce the notion of both dimensions affecting each other.

CHACKAK (engraving): Stand with your arms at your sides. Steadily raise them above your head with your palms facing and your thumbs pointing out. Lower them again and repeat ten times.

CHATZAV (cutting): Raise both arms above your head. With fingertips touching, bring your arms down in a chopping motion. Raise them again and repeat ten times.

TSARAF (welding): Stretch your arms out in front, then pull them back and out to the sides as far as you can. Steadily bring them together as though compressing something. Open them again and repeat ten times.

SHAKAL (weighing): Lower your arms to your sides, with your palms facing forward. Raise your arms to chest level as if lifting. Lower again and repeat ten times.

HEMIR (exchanging): Stretch your arms out to the sides, with your palms facing forward. Simultaneously bring each hand to the opposite shoulder. Open and repeat ten times.

By Abulafia, based on Sefer Yetzirah 2.2

experience the presence of God, as opposed to simply recognizing it.

Abulafia focused heavily on the Hebrew alphabet, suggesting that it was the vehicle through which we can ascend toward God. Anyone could meditate on the shapes of the letters to arouse intuitive capabilities, while their sounds could open up the channels of communication between God and Man.

Abulafia also expanded the ideas of Nachmanides. The Kabbalah was not just a way for an individual to develop spiritually but also a means of righting the evils of the world and removing the scars of exile from the Jewish people.

Abulafia's influence was great, and this led some to oppose him. In Rome in 1280 Pope Nicholas III imprisoned him and sentenced him to death for heresy. But the Pope died before the sentence could be carried out, and Abulafia was released. He wrote his last work, *Imre Shefer* (*Words of Beauty*), around 1290, after which all trace of him is lost.

The last line of a Haggadah, which reads, "Next year in Jerusalem."

Moses de León

Moses Ben Shem Tov de León is one of the most influential of all Kabbalists. He was born in León in Castile around 1250 and is the person who brought the *Zohar* to the attention of the world.

Moses de León was a prolific writer on the Kabbalah both in Hebrew and in a form of Aramaic unique to the mystics. Among his works are: the *Sefer HaRimmon*, an explanation of the mystical significance of the ritual commandments of the *Torah*; *Mishkan Ha'eydut*, on the soul after death; and *Maskiyot Kessef*, an explanation of the significance of prayers.

In the 1290s, while living in Guadalajara, de León started publishing sections of a text entitled the *Zohar* (Brightness). It is still disputed whether he wrote this text or compiled it from different sources; or whether, as he claimed, he simply discovered and disseminated a work by the great mystic Shimon Ben Yochai, who had lived 1,000 years earlier. De León denied writing the manuscript. But no-one else ever saw the original, and his wife claimed that there never was one.

Despite the reservations of sceptics, the *Zohar* has become the most important Jewish mystical text, even among the orthodox community. Many rabbis have accepted it as more authoritative than any other post-talmudic source on religious thoughts and interpretations – even on matters of Jewish law.

On the transmigration of souls, for example, the *Zohar* suggests that the souls of the righteous return to Heaven each night to be "inspired" by the divine light. Others remain mired in the physical. After death all souls return to be judged by God, then are sent back to the human world. While good souls bring past goodness with them, the bad bring their bad experiences back to Earth.

Joseph Gikatilla

One of de León's best-known pupils was Joseph Gikatilla (1248–c.1325). Their partnership was one of the most productive in the history of the Kabbalah.

Gikatilla's best-known work is *Ginat Egoz* (*The Nut Garden*), written in 1274. In this he formulated a method called *zeruf* (fusion), a way of combining letters, vowels and sounds to reveal the true names of God and release spiritual energy.

Gikatilla also applied the *sefirot* to human beings therapeutically. If God can be represented by the *sefirot* and Man is created in the divine image, then it would follow that a human being has parallel qualities which need to be nurtured for him to function effectively. Gikatilla drew on Maimonides and Abulafia to devise physical exercises – not unlike those of tai chi – that would achieve balance in body and mind.

The Zohar

The Zohar is the central book of the Kabbalah, but also one of the most influential in all Judaism. Far from being overly magical, it is a magisterial, consciously nonrational commentary on the *Torah*.

The Zohar (*Brightness*) is a compilation of texts. The main body is a detailed commentary on the *Five Books of Moses*: Genesis, Exodus and Leviticus, Numbers up to chapter 26, and a few fragments from Deuteronomy. In addition there are three major "lectures" — the *Idra Rabbah* (*Great Gathering*), *Idra Zuta* (*Small Gathering*) and

"When he began creating the world, the Heavenly King allowed supernatural brightness to emerge from the limitlessness, and it sowed a secret seed, like a silkworm enclosing itself in a palace, called Elohim, and out of Elohim everything emerged. This is what is meant by 'The Beginning Created Elohim.'"

ZOHAR I.54A

the *Raya Mehemna* (Honest Shepherd) — as well as around 12 other "lectures" or booklets (different editions include different extra texts).

All the books are written in Aramaic and share the style and content of a mystical novel. They do not deal with the literal meaning of the traditional holy texts but treat almost everything transcendentally, above and beyond time and space.

Rabbi Shimon wanders through Galilee with his companions, commenting on the personalities they meet. Characters of the *Bible* represent different aspects of God. There are epic struggles between good and evil. Slavery in Egypt is the slavery of the soul trapped in the body. The structure and ceremonies of the Tabernacle are symbolic and show us how to respond to God and bring His energy down to Earth.

A page from the 14th-century Barcelona Haggadah, showing Hebrew slaves building for the Egpytian Pharaoh.

ZOHAR IDEAS AND PRACTICES

The *Zohar* contains many different and
sometimes contradictory ideas. It is more a
compendium than a systematic theology,
and is used by many Jewish people today
as a source of inspiration and meditation,
as well as material for daily study.

Emanation and the *Sefirot*

Mysticism has always tried to explain how a nonphysical, infinite being called God can interact with the material world and with physical human beings with limited capacities. Jewish mysticism answered this through the theory of *sefirot*.

The idea of *sefirot* has been repeatedly reworked throughout the history of the Kabbalah. This is a simplified version that emerges from the pages of the *Zohar*.

To understand God we need to talk about His essence. But we humans are incapable of grasping something that is beyond the physical world. So God "emanates": He distils Himself into forms that are more readily accessible to us but are not actually His essence. The *sefirot* are, in a sense, like radio waves that

carry His voice to us, as long as we have an appropriate receiver with which to receive the signals.

The *Talmud* uses the term *Schechina* (Presence) to describe His interface with humanity. In the *Zohar*, *Schechina* is associated with just one of the ten *sefirot* which comprise the link between us and the unknowable *Ein Sof*. The *sefirot* are not

Opposite: A depiction of the Tree of Life, carved on a synagogue in Prague.

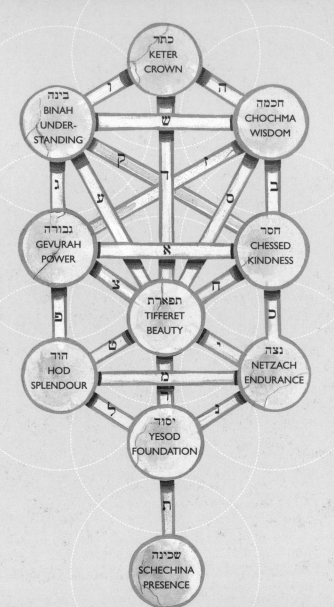

Feminine aspects

BINAH
YHVH (ELOHIM)
HEAD (INTUITIVE
KNOWLEDGE)

GEVURAH
ELOHIM
RIGHT ARM
DIN (JUDGMENT)

HOD
ELOHIM TZEVAOT
RIGHT THIGH

YESOD
SHADDAI
REPRODUCTIVE ORGANS

SCHECHINA
ADONAI
FEET
MALCHUT (KINGDOM)

Masculine aspects

KETER
EHYH ASHR EHYH
HEAD (WILL)
AYIN (NOTHINGNESS)

CHOCHMA
YAH
HEAD (COGNITIVE
KNOWLEDGE)

CHESSED
EL
LEFT ARM
GEDULLA (LOVE)

TIFFERET
YHVH (ADONAI)
HEART
RACHAMIM (COMPASSION)

NETZACH
ADONAI TZEVAOT
LEFT THIGH

כתר
KETER
CROWN

בינה
BINAH
UNDER-
STANDING

חכמה
CHOCHMA
WISDOM

גבורה
GEVURAH
POWER

חסד
CHESSED
KINDNESS

תפארת
TIFFERET
BEAUTY

הוד
HOD
SPLENDOUR

נצח
NETZACH
ENDURANCE

יסוד
YESOD
FOUNDATION

שכינה
SCHECHINA
PRESENCE

distinct — from God, each other or our world — so the term "emanate" is used to imply a continuum.

The ten qualities of God are ideas rather than entities. Kabbalists often disagree as to their exact names and order, so what follows is a general description. At the top is *Keter* (Crown). This is followed by *Chochma* (Wisdom), then *Binah* (Understanding). These top three are the intellectual *sefirot*, closer to the source of pure *Ein Sof* than the other seven, which are closer to God's physical presence. Next come *Chessed* (Kindness) and *Gevurah* (Power). Between these and lower down

Opposite: The sefirot depicted in a "Tree of Life" formation. The labels at the sides list, in order, the name of God, part of the body and any alternative name (in italics) associated with each sefira.

is *Tifferet* (Beauty). Next are *Netzach* (Endurance) and *Hod* (Splendour). Then down and back is *Yesod* (Foundation). Finally comes *Schechina* (Presence). The *sefirot* are divided equally into masculine and feminine aspects.

God is multifaceted, and each *sefira* has a specific name of God attached to it. However, humans are made in the divine image, so every aspect of the Divine is also mirrored in every aspect of our spiritual sensitivity. When we suffer, for example, we experience God one way; when we are happy we experience Him another. Sometimes we are self-reliant and sometimes we need support; sometimes we are judged and sometimes shown mercy. We may encounter God intellectually or emotionally.

The *sefirot* are interconnected through channels of energy, each of which is represented by a letter of the Hebrew alphabet. When there is an imbalance in our own qualities, these channels of energy can help us to rectify it. For example, if you are feeling too aggressive and so weighted toward *Gevurah* (Power), meditating on the letter *Aleph*, which links *Gevurah* to *Chessed* (Kindness), would help you to redress the balance.

Restoring balance in ourselves also helps to restore equilibrium in the world as a whole – and ultimately helps to establish harmony with the Divine. Failure to do so explains the imperfections in our world.

The *sefirot* are depicted in various formations. The "tree" shape (as shown on page 60) is based on the imagery in *Psalm* 1 of a pious person likened to a tree. The tree draws nourishment through its leaves as well as through its roots. This is the imagery of *Etz Chayim* (*Tree of Life*), usually associated with the *Torah*. In the Kabbalah the *Torah* encompasses both God speaking to humanity and humanity speaking to God.

The *sefirot* are also often shown in human form, with each *sefira* associated with a different part of the anatomy. In practical mysticism these physical *sefirot* are used like chakras and acupuncture points: focusing on different parts of the body can help us to access different types of energy. On a lower level the *sefirot* can help humans to understand themselves. The Zohar tells us that if we don't know how we function, we cannot begin to approach God. The *Bible* says we are made "in the image of God", so our spiritual journey starts within ourselves.

There is also a connection between the ten *sefirot* and creation. In *Genesis* God says "Let there be …" ten times during the process of creation. This led to the later idea that it might be possible to use the *sefirot* to create life.

As they are multidimensional, the *sefirot* are also identified with each measure of time – hours, days, months and every religious occasion. They represent the way in which divine energy permeates the whole universe. They show that we are each a world in ourselves and yet everyone is interconnected and part of a greater whole.

The sefirot in human form, often referred to as Adam Kadmon (primordial Man).

Divine Names

Each aspect of God has a different name, which illustrates the different ways of perceiving and experiencing the Divine. And, as everything in the Kabbalah is both male and female, so, too, does God have masculine and feminine aspects.

In the *Bible* names reveal something about the inner nature of a person and of God. Moses asked God to reveal His name and God replied with "EHYH AShR EHYH" ("I am that I am"). This combination is a clue to many later kabbalistic formulations of the divine name. (In Hebrew the word EHYH can also be understood to mean "past", "present" and "future".) It also led to the essential four-letter name of God, YHVH – sometimes known as the Tetragrammaton.

YHVH was pronounced only once a year by the High Priest in the Temple, and then it was pronounced *Adonai*. In a normal religious context, YHVH is referred to with the term *Hashem* (The Name).

In the *Bible* there are seven different names for God. Each has a specific significance. For example, the name *Elohim* also means "judges" in biblical Hebrew, so this name is associated with God judging humanity. Early mystics would refer to God using a different biblical

name depending on the context. These biblical names are sacred and not to be used casually. In talmudic times new names were created for daily use, including *Ribbono Shel Olam* (Master of the Universe) and *Hakadosh Baruch Hu* (Holy One, Blessed Be He).

The Kabbalists were the first to link the biblical names of God to the *sefirot*

Reading from right to left, the Hebrew for Ein Sof (Infinite God).

(see page 60) and would weave meditations on these names into existing prayers. To emphasize other qualities of God in their writings, they initiated the use of terms such as *Ein Sof* (Infinite God) and *Partzufim* (Faces of God).

ההההההההההההה

Meditation using God's Name

Taken from an anonymous 16th-century commentary on the *Zohar*, this meditation shows

us how to look at the letters of God's name and imagine them conveying God's power.

God's name is made up of the letters *Yod, Vav, Hey*.

Look at the letter *Hey* before your eyes.

The letter *Hey* is composed of a *Daled* and a *Yod*.

The *Daled* is the door.

Yod is the key to the door.

Daled is made up of a *Vav* across the top of another *Vav*.

Yod opens the two *Vavs*.

Each letter of God is a door that opens to the other.

Hey is the womb that *Yod* fertilizes to create the world.

From Shaar HaSod

ההההההההההההה

The Kabbalists also invented entirely new "names" for God by combining letters from crucial biblical texts. The Zohar mentions the 70-letter (or 72-letter) name of God, which is made up of the initial letters of the 35 words of *Genesis*, chapter 2, verses 1 to 3, repeated. This 70-letter name formed the basis of meditations used during prayer. Later mystics developed similar "names" from other significant texts and used them to add layers of meaning to the original scripture.

There is another important aspect of the divine names. In *Genesis 1* God creates man and woman in the image of God. So the Zohar divides the *sefirot*, and their associated divine names, into male and female aspects (see page 60). We can direct our prayers to whichever we feel to be more appropriate.

More than anything, the Zohar stresses the importance of pronouncing the divine names; and although the book does not provide specific meditations, contemporary Kabbalists began to place a greater emphasis on practical mysticism. People started to seek the "right" permutation of letters, which, if said correctly, would open up a direct channel of communication with God.

Arranged in this form (a tetracys), the letters YHVH add up to 72. This can be used as a charm or as a focus for prayer.

Creation

Medieval philosophers assumed that God made the world out of nothing. But the mystics could not countenance the idea of a God totally distinct from the physical world. They envisioned the world made out of God, so that everything is, in a way, divine.

In the Middle Ages many theologians described God as the "Prime Mover" — that which was there before anything else and started the process of creation. They called this process *creatio ex nihilo* (creation out of nothing). However, this idea prompted people to question the

Opposite: Creation, as shown in a 15th-century Haggadah, beginning top right with the division of light and dark, and ending with a man resting on the Sabbath.

relationship between God, the universe and mankind. Was it possible that God, having made the world, had withdrawn again, and that His detachment had allowed evil into the world?

Jewish mystics could not accept this idea. They asserted that there was an inextricable link between God and his creation. Some thought pantheistically: God and the universe were one and the same. But most saw God as a total, concentrated being, one who although

> "… the Divine King sent out a filament of great light, a flashing streak of immeasurable brightness from the impenetrable depths of the mysterious and endless space. Then Ein Sof measured and fashioned this bright light and it radiated outward and created a division between itself and everything beyond, remaining itself unknowable. This was the reyshit (the beginning), the creative expression of the Divine Will, the starting-point of everything."
>
> **ZOHAR I.15A**

somehow removed from the universe, was constantly involved in sustaining it.

There were, however, differing explanations as to how the world was created. According to *Midrash* (talmudic commentary on the *Bible*), God created successive worlds and destroyed them until He produced this one. The opening of *Genesis* relates how the spirit of God hovered over the chaos and then formed the waters and then the Earth. Creation was therefore a kind of distillation: God's spirit was distilled through air, fire and water into the Earth.

The *Bahir* suggested that God created the world by placing layers of material over Himself. When we look and see matter, this is only superficial. If we could peel the surface away, we would realize that the world is God. This, of course, has implications for our behaviour: everything in the universe must be treated with sanctity.

The Zohar was far more innovative. In Hebrew the opening phrase of Genesis reads: "In the beginning God created." In the Zohar this was reworked to read, "The beginning created God." First there was Ein Sof, the infinite, nonmaterial God. Ein Sof emitted a beam of creative energy to produce Elohim, the God who is present in the universe and the first God mentioned in the Bible. Elohim was, in a sense, fertilized by this beam of supernatural energy – the Zohar of the book's title – to produce the Heavens, the Earth and all life. So God created the world out of an emanation, a distillation of His own divine energy.

This creative process is reflected in the symbolism of God's name, Elohim. In Hebrew this name is represented by the letter Hey, which is shaped like a womb with two entrances. The Zohar suggests that Hey was fertilized by Yod, one of the other three letters of God's name, and that this produced the world.

The idea that creation was manifested through holy language is conveyed in Genesis in the phrase "Let there be …" which is repeated ten times and is the origin of the ten sefirot.

From the 13th century onward, some Kabbalists started to understand the process of creation as it was described in the Zohar in terms of the Tree of Life – the continuing interactive relationship between God and the Earth reflecting the way in which a tree is nourished through its leaves and roots.

Souls

Rationalist Jewish thinkers believed that the soul was destructible. The Zohar suggests that there is a number of eternal souls, whose task it is to reform humanity.

The Zohar's ideas on the soul may at first seem contradictory. Souls are "recycled" until humanity is reformed. However, everyone also has a unique soul. This can be explained if we think that, just as our bodies are made up of earlier genetic material, so, too, are our souls made up of previous souls. Thus some souls are spiritually richer at birth than others. Some, however, are made from the sitra achra – the negative aspect of creation.

The Bible uses three words for soul: nefesh (life force), ruach (spirit), and neshama (breath of life). The Talmud added ot (living essence) and yechida (unity). The Zohar expands on these descriptions. Nefesh is the lifeblood that distinguishes living creatures from dead. Ruach is the intellect. Neshama is exclusively concerned with communing with God – a built-in faculty that is able to "experience the divine presence". The ot was the soul that is "beyond language" and is our connection to the source of life. Finally, the yechida is closest to the divine origins of creation in Ein Sof.

Good and Evil

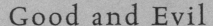

The *Zohar* does not accept the idea of "original sin". Evil in the universe, such as a natural disaster, arises out of the residue from the process of creation. Evil in humans is a result of free will.

Thinkers had for centuries been concerned with the question of why a world created by God was not perfect. The *Zohar* gives three kinds of answers. The first is that God had made and destroyed many worlds before he refined chaos into the matter of this world. However, this process left over a residue, called *klippot* (shells). These impure *klippot* cause evil in the world.

The second idea was that God has two aspects. Gnostic thinkers believed in two Gods, one good and one evil – the latter often identified with the devil. The mystics of Gerona had developed this to say that just as God shows different qualities in the *sefirot* (such as judgment and mercy), so too can each of God's qualities be understood in

> "When God created Man, He asked that Man only follow Him with single-minded faith. But then they turned aside, abandoned that special tree which is higher than all other trees and they preferred the place which is constantly changing from colour to colour, from good to bad and bad to good. They preferred the changeable and abandoned the supreme and changeless One. That is why their hearts alternated between good and bad and why they sometimes deserved mercy and sometimes punishment, according to their actions."

ZOHAR 3.107B

another way – judgment may sometimes feel harsh. The Zohar suggested that evil was more removed from God by giving a name to this negative aspect: *sitra achra* (the "other side"). When we draw our energies from the *sitra achra*, we act in an evil way. God does not contain evil: it is a question of how we use His energies.

The third idea concerns the Tree of Life and the Tree of Knowledge in the Garden of Eden. Originally these trees were united, but when Man made the wrong decisions, they were separated. This took things further from the original perfection of creation. Imperfection enabled evil to enter the world.

Adam and Eve

The Zohar treats Adam and Eve as equal, two sides (*partzufim*) of one being, made both male and female in the image of God. Division of the *partzufim* leads to discord or sin.

In *Genesis*, chapter 1, mankind is a "male and female" being. The names Adam and Eve are not used until chapter 2, perhaps to reflect the growing complexity of the world, and possibly to indicate that choice had entered their world. When mankind made the wrong choice, sin came into being. This event is indicated in the Zohar, which

Adam and Eve in an illustration from a Hebrew Bible, c.1280. Evil seeks to keep them divided from each other and from God.

> "Any image that does not embrace male and female
> is not a high and true image. ...
> A human being is only called Adam
> when male and female are as one."
>
> **ZOHAR, RAYA MEHEMNA, 2B**

refers to the perfect sinless human — Adam and Eve — as *Adam Kadmon* (primordial Man). After the Fall *Adam Kadmon* is known as *Adam Belial* (destructive Man).

The only way that Adam and Eve can compensate the world for the loss of perfection is by reuniting with God. To achieve this they must reconcile their two *partzufim* and restore Man to God's image. This goal is symbolized by their first sexual union in the Garden of Eden, which was perfect, without shame — and which mirrored the creative union inherent in the *sefirot*.

Naturally, this account lays itself open to misconstruction, and some Kabbalists were excommunicated for promiscuity. The *Zohar*, like the rest of the Kabbalah, was concerned to emphasize a holistic outlook. Union is not only physical, but also spiritual. All actions, including sexual ones, should include a mystical dimension, and all mystical actions should involve the whole body.

Angels

The *Zohar* describes how on the first day God created good angels out of divine light. Other, less benevolent angels were created on the second day out of fire. All angels work under God's authority.

There are four archangels who preside over the human world: Michael, the angel of mercy; Gabriel, the angel of fire and war; Uriel (or Nuriel), the angel of divine light; and Raphael, the angel of healing. They act as God's messengers in the sense that they channel His will down to Earth and help us to access His

> "*A person's birth is accompanied by four angels: Michael stands for Abraham; Gabriel for Isaac; Nuriel for Jacob; and Raphael for Adam. But if the person has no tradition of goodness, the four powers of evil accompany the birth: anger, destruction, immorality and impatience.*"
>
> **ZOHAR, RAYA MEHEMNA, 4B**

energy. They represent the choices and opportunities we have in life.

Another important angel is Metatron, whose role is some-what ambiguous. He influences intellectual activity, but is also devoid of spirit, and able to lead us into profane study.

Beneath these high-ranking angels is a vast order of lower angels, who preside over more specific aspects of our world, such as hours, days, animals, even stones and blades of grass.

Lower still, ranking between the angels and humans, are the bad angels. They are not evil in themselves but allow negative energies into the world, which we have to try to resist. (This echoes the use of the word "satan" in the *Bible*: it often means simply "obstacle" or the "other side".) One of the most striking

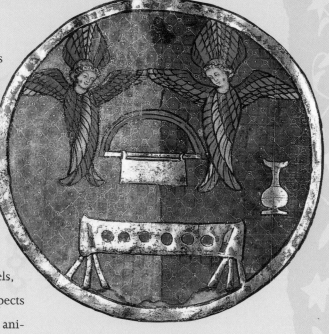

Angels guard the Ark of the Covenant, which contains God's word, the Torah.

of these figures is Lilith, the female spirit of the night, who is portrayed as a seducer of men and murderer of children. However, this should not be taken to mean that women are associated with evil – this idea is alien to the *Zohar*.

Meditation and Prayer

Early mysticism saw obedience to the commandments as the primary method of connecting with God. Meditation and prayer were always thought of as supplementary. However, over the course of time, prayer came to play a more important role.

The Hebrew word *kavvanah* means "focusing" or "preparation". The mystics of Gerona applied the term to exercises that they devised in order to prepare themselves for prayer.

Most *kavvanot* involved meditation. For example, mystics might create a new name of God from the initial letters of a psalm. This name would serve as a mental and/or visual focus, helping the mystic to concentrate his mind on God and on his own actions. Over time some people began to credit such names with magical powers, like those of amulets.

Kavvanot are described in the *Zohar* as a way of elevating the soul toward Heaven, closer to God. These meditations ensure that when we pray, we are not simply asking God to come down to Earth to answer our mundane requests. The mystics believed that *kavvanot* could give them an existential experience of God, much like standing in the wind to experience nature.

> "When a man begins the evening prayer, an eagle comes down and takes up his prayers on its wings. This angel is Nuriel when it comes from Chessed (Kindness), and Uriel when it comes from the side of Gevurah (Power), because then it is like a burning fire."
>
> **ZOHAR I.23B**

Mystics of this time would engage in two types of prayer: some structured and formal, based on the established liturgy; some more fluid, spontaneous and personal. The *Zohar* emphasized the power of this latter type. The first stage of such prayer can "correct" and "restore" the person who is praying. If this succeeds, that person can go on to rectify the physical Lower World that we inhabit. With continued prayer it is possible to influence the Higher World of the angels and spirits. Eventually prayer can enable a person to reach God by discovering and using the "correct" divine name. People who achieved this level of spirituality became known as *Baal Shem Tov* (Masters of the Good Name) and were said to be able to change the world.

Later mystics in Safed (see page 102) developed informal prayer into group meditation. They would get the whole community to concentrate on elevating itself and correcting the global order.

Meditation before the Sabbath Prayer

Although this prayer from the *Zohar* is sometimes sung, it was intended for silent meditation in preparation for Friday night services in the synagogue.

The secret of the Sabbath is in the Sabbath itself which is created out of the unity of the perfect yet hidden God.

This prayer as we enter the Sabbath expresses the secret of the unity of God as we experience it through His precious throne.

The Sabbath was ordained to enable us to elevate ourselves toward the Holy King on High.

As the Sabbath comes in, it scatters the negative forces of the "other side".

And all its powers are cancelled out through the holiness of the Divine Spirit.

Everything material is crowned with the divine crowns of the Holy Spirit.

All negative powers, all fear of judgment and punishment, are transported from this world to the other,

And divine energy suffuses the lower world of God's holy followers.

They are all suffused with new and pure souls that enable them to delight in the presence of Heaven.

מקשה הוא כמראה אשר הראה

CHAPTER FOUR

THEMES AND SYMBOLS

The Kabbalah touches on all aspects of life,
and mystics illustrated this in discussions on
numerous themes including astrology, sexuality
and dreams. Symbols, such as amulets and the
menorah, were used as aids for prayer and
contemplation, to protect and to cure, and
to encourage devotion and speculation.

Astrology

Although soothsaying was forbidden in the *Bible*, astrology was important to Jewish mystics – less as a method of prediction than as a way of aiding and explaining human behaviour.

Everything in the universe is made up of divine energy, a mixture of physical and spiritual. A soul, for example, is part of a wider universal soul. A body is made up of particles that are linked to others. Kabbalists interpret this in different ways. Some suggest that because everything is connected in this way, the stars and planets can influence our moods and behaviour. Others would say that the zodiac does not have as much power as this, but is more symbolic of the various energies of the universe. Humans have

free will, and by acting in a spiritual way, such as following the *Torah*, a person can rise above the lesser influence of the stars and strengthen the influence of the greater divine energy.

The astrological system was first discussed at length in the *Sefer Yetzirah* (*Book of Creation*), which associates the planets with the *sefirot* and with the human organs. Over time the system became more and more complex, linking the universal signs of the zodiac to the 12 tribes of Israel, the months of the Jewish

year, the single letters of the Hebrew alphabet (see page 17) and the hours of the day. The seven planets were linked to the days of the week, the number of orifices in the head, the double letters of the Hebrew alphabet, the firmaments, and the universes, seas and deserts.

To take one example, the planet Saturn is associated with Friday, the first hour of the day, the left nostril, the letter

The zodiac can help to explain moods and actions, but is not used for prediction.

Reysh and peace. So someone who was in search of peace might fast, meditate or pray on the first hour of Friday, focusing on the letter Reysh, the left nostril and Saturn. However, not all Kabbalists would agree on just how effective such action might be.

Amulets

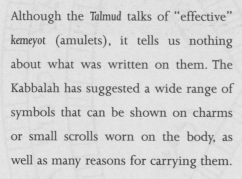

Amulets date back to the earliest times. In an orthodox context they were simply used as reminders of the constant and healing presence of God. But the Kabbalah gives them additional powers, not just to heal but also to reach the Divine.

Although the *Talmud* talks of "effective" *kemeyot* (amulets), it tells us nothing about what was written on them. The Kabbalah has suggested a wide range of symbols that can be shown on charms or small scrolls worn on the body, as well as many reasons for carrying them.

The hand symbol is a common image in North Africa, used to ward off the Evil Eye – often an image of an eye was placed in the palm. The name of Joseph is invoked to help to overcome the Evil

Eye because Joseph managed to resist the Pharaoh's wife's attempts to seduce him – "his eye did not wish to benefit from that which did not belong to him".

Charms in the shape of squares and rectangles are also common. They generally include quotations from the *Bible* but also contain shapes and symbols that originally had magical provenance but were adapted by Kabbalists to represent angelic energy. Such charms are worn about the person, either over or under

clothing. Some were made to place on wounds or to cure certain illnesses.

The six-pointed Star of David was not widely used as a symbol until relatively late, in the Middle Ages. It may well owe its popularity to being a variation on the magical pentangle. Around the star or in its angles would be the names of God or a specific prayer or formula.

One particular type of charm is the *shiviti* – a name that comes from the line in *Psalm 16*: "I have placed [*shiviti*] God before me all the time." A *shiviti* is decorated with symbols and names of God and hung on a synagogue lectern or on the walls of the home as a focal point for meditation or prayer.

Some charms, such as this 18th-century parchment, were written on tiny scrolls that could be carried around.

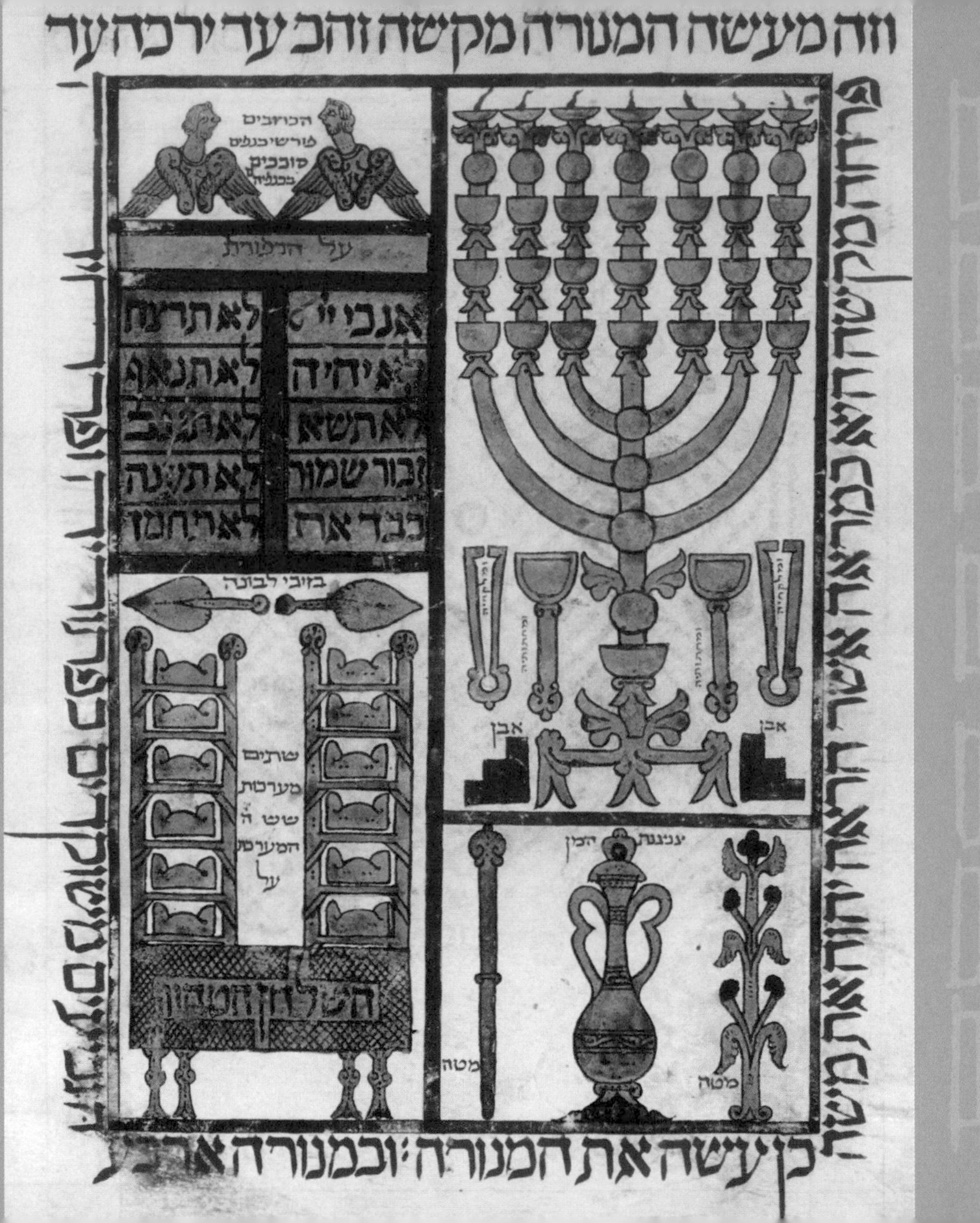

וזה מעשה המנרה מקשה זהב עד ירכה עד
הכרובים
על הכפורת
אנכי יי
לא יהיה
לא תשא
זכור שמור
כבד את
לא תרצח
לא תנאף
לא תגנב
לא תענה
לא תחמד
בזיכי לבונה
שתים
מערכות
שש
המערכת
על
השלחן
אבן
אבן
צנצנת המן
מטה
מטה
כן עשה את המנורה ׃ וכמנורה

The Menorah

The seven-branched and three-legged candelabrum, described in *Exodus* as an essential part of the Tabernacle and later the Temple, is an important mystical symbol in both structure and function.

In the *Bible* God often appears to humans in the form of fire – a suggestive symbol, as fire warms but can also destroy. The westernmost light on the candelabrum in the Temple was kept burning permanently as a symbol of God's presence, and in every synagogue today the "eternal light" burns above the Ark which holds the scrolls of the *Torah*.

Opposite: A Bible illumination depicting ritual temple objects c.1300, including a menorah, top right.

Mystics combined the symbolism of fire with the significant number of "branches" on the *menorah*: including the legs, the total of ten has an obvious association with the ten *sefirot*. So the *menorah* came to represent keeping the tradition alive and bringing the presence of the *sefirot* to a position of prominence before our eyes. The candelabrum appears as a motif in drawings embellished with mystical formulae, which were placed before a Kabbalist conducting prayers and used as an aid for concentration.

Numbers

The *Talmud* talks of *gematria* (numerology), but the art dates back much further — it was mentioned by Pythagoras (c.580–500 BCE). In the Kabbalah *gematria* is another means of communing with God.

Each letter of the Hebrew alphabet has a numerical value (see page 17), which means that the total value of words can convey additional meanings and connections. The Hebrew word SHFT (judge), for example, has the same numerical value as TFHS (fool).

In talmudic times *gematria* was used to uncover links between the words of the *Torah*. The Kabbalah took this interest further and the numbers acquired special significance. The most common letters used in the many names of God are Hey,

five, and *Yod*, ten. The *sefirot* are divided into two sets of five, male and female.

Three and seven are also important. Three "mother" letters connect the *sefirot*: *Aleph*, *Mem* and *Shin*, symbolizing the primordial elements (air, water and fire). The Sabbath is the seventh day, while the festival of *Yom Kippur* (Day of Atonement) falls in the seventh month. The ten *sefirot* comprise three of the mind and seven of the body. Numbers like this could be used in meditation as a way of uncovering the path to God.

231 Gates Meditation

In this meditation there are two circles, each showing all the letters of the Hebrew alphabet. By revolving the outer circle against the inner, you create different letter and number combinations. Each of the possible 231 permutations is a gate to divine energy.

Sit or stand facing Jerusalem. Imagine that you are in the centre of a circle and around you is a series of arches, like the Colosseum in Rome. Inside each arch, or gate, is a letter of the Hebrew alphabet, starting with *Aleph* in front of you.

Envision another circle of gates inside the first circle. Inside each gate is a letter of the Hebrew alphabet, starting with *Aleph* in front of you.

Revolve the outer *Aleph* round to align with the inner *Bet* gate, then with the inner *Gimmel* gate and so on, until you complete the circle.

Repeat the exercise, but start with with the outer *Bet* gate. Ignore same letter or inverted combinations, such as *Bet–Bet*, or *Aleph–Bet* and *Bet–Aleph*. Continue until you complete the circle.

Repeat with each letter of the outer circle until you complete the entire sequence.

As you repeat this meditation, some combinations of letters may strike you as more powerful than others. Try focusing your meditation on them: eventually you may find the one that is your personal portal to divine energy.

Sexuality

The traditional Jewish view of sexuality has always been very positive, but the Kabbalah gives sexuality a special place in unifying the physical and the spiritual worlds. Harnessing this power can help us to get closer to God.

Kabbalistic theory sees both the physical and the mystical world as being composed of male and female dimensions that are equal. When mankind was created it was as both male and female. The later version of the story, which portrays Eve coming from the rib of Adam, was designed to emphasize their close emotional relationship – the rib cage contains the heart, the symbol of love. More importantly, the union of these dimensions is a creative one: Ein Sof "fertilized" Elohim (see page 71) to create the world. On Earth human sexual union mirrors this divine creative union.

The kabbalistic approach to sexuality is a holistic one. On one level this means that sex should involve intellectual, emotional, moral and spiritual aspects. More profoundly, it also means that sexual pleasure is a legitimate means of getting closer to God.

Each of the sefirot is essential to fulfilling human potential and experiencing

God. The central lower *sefira*, *Yesod*, is the symbol for sexual creativity. But it is inextricably linked to all the other *sefirot*, and any function involving *Yesod* must involve the other *sefirot* in order to be effective. Also, *Yesod* and sexuality are just as important as, say, *Chochma* and intellect as a way of connecting to God. Failure to connect physically is as inadequate as failure to connect mentally.

Mystics suggest that we can unite with God by "marrying" the Sabbath Bride. This means enjoying the Sabbath like a bride, on a physical and spiritual level.

This idea was distorted by some Kabbalists such as Jacob Frank, who argued that frequent sex could help us to achieve spiritual heights. He was excommunicated for heresy.

The Yearly Cycle

The yearly cycle of Jewish festivals represents the various kinds of relationship that exist between Man and God. Kabbalists added their own layers of rituals and symbols.

The festival of *Pesach* (Passover) relates to the Exodus from Egypt. Mystically it is seen as the soul's escape from slavery. Egypt is the *sitra achra* (the "other side"). The *matzah* bread eaten during *Pesach* represents the soul that is unleavened when pure but puffs up with sin. The *seder* (Passover meal) is celebrated in white garments, which are a sign of simple poverty, saintliness and death.

Shavuot (Pentecost) celebrates the giving of the *Torah* at Mount Sinai. In mystical terms it represents the "marriage"

A 14th-century Spanish representation of the seder held at Passover.

between God and Israel. The Jewish people assented to this contract, and the relationship is consummated each time we worship God using the language and guidelines of the *Torah*.

Sukkot (Tabernacles) is based on the temporary shelters the Israelites built as they wandered in the desert. It establishes the marital home of God and humanity. According to the *Zohar*, the souls of Abraham, Isaac, Jacob, Moses, Aaron, Joseph and King David, collectively known as the *Ushpizzin* (guests), should be invited to join in the festival.

Rosh Hashanah (New Year) is the time at which the heavenly cycles unite with the earthly cycles – the seven heavens with the seven seas, rivers and continents. This is when we should all start the process of purifying ourselves by submitting to divine will with the same commitment as Isaac who allowed himself to be bound and prepared for sacrifice.

Yom Kippur (Day of Atonement) is the final opportunity to perfect the mystical union between Man and God. It requires the total denial of the material world through fasting.

Above: A liturgical calendar showing cycles of years. Every seventh year was sabbatical and no agricultural work was done.

Dreams

Throughout the Jewish tradition dreams have played an important role in revealing the heavenly world to humans. They are a way in which God can commune with us.

In sleep our souls can ascend to the spiritual realm and receive nourishment.

The *Bible* tells us that God appeared to Abraham and Jacob in dreams. Joseph's dreams foretold the future, and he, in turn, interpreted the Pharaoh's dreams. The traditional attitude of rabbis varied from those who saw dreams as messages from God to those who saw them simply as reflections of the workings of the human mind.

In the mystical tradition the *Hasidei Ashkenaz* (Pious Men of Germany) saw dreams as vehicles for God's glory, and introduced penances for anyone who

> "When a person is sleeping in bed, the soul leaves the body and floats toward
> the higher world and meets pure spirits. If she is worthy, she sees important
> and wonderful things, but if not, she falls into the hands of the 'other side'
> who tell her lies about what will happen shortly. When the person wakes,
> the soul communicates what she saw. The bad person recalls a happy dream,
> but it is not true. And that person will be misled further from the truth."
>
> **ZOHAR I.183A**

disturbed them. The Kabbalah upholds this regard for dream life. In the *Zohar* prophecy is seen as a "masculine" vehicle for transmitting God's will, whereas dreams are a "feminine" vehicle – their messages are somehow softer and more emotional. The content of dreams, however, is important: some tell the future; others inspire religious poetry; some can even influence legal decisions.

Those seeking to understand a dream can appeal for inspiration from the archangel Gabriel, who is responsible for distributing dreams. However, the *Zohar* warns that some dreams can be false. As it is possible that an interpretation could become a self-fulfilling prophecy, only an expert – such as a teacher, rabbi or *Baal Shem Tov* – should attempt to decipher dreams.

CHAPTER FIVE

THE MIDDLE EAST

Expulsion of the Jews from Spain in 1492

resulted in a mass movement east. It also

changed the direction of mystic thought.

The emphasis shifted from individual to national

issues of guilt, penance and redemption.

Messianism and universal *tikkun* (repair)

became central to kabbalistic thought.

Safed

After being forced out of Spain in 1492, a wave of highly talented and cultural Jews moved eastward to Italy, Greece, Turkey and Israel. The town of Safed, overlooking the Sea of Galilee, soon became the hub of kabbalistic thought and practice.

Many exiles were attracted to Jerusalem, but it had no industry and could not support a large community. The nearby town of Safed, however, had a vibrant textile industry and offered a refuge.

From around 1530 two great scholars of *halakha* (Jewish law), Jacob Berab and Joseph Caro, were established in Safed. Their community lived a holy life and waited for the Messiah. It was here that Moses Alkabetz wrote the mystic poem *Lekhah Dodi* (*Come, My Beloved*), which was sung in the fields at sunset to greet the Sabbath Bride. But it was Moses Cordovero who ensured Safed's place in the history of the Kabbalah.

MOSES CORDOVERO

In addition to being a remarkable teacher and a powerful personality, Moses Cordovero was a deep thinker and theorist, who collected and summarized all the teachings of the Kabbalah up to that time.

In Pardess Rimmonim (Orchard of Pomegranates), Cordovero reworked ideas about the *sefirot*, suggesting that they were not so much part of a process of emanation from God but more like independent agents of dynamic renewal. Rather than viewing the *sefirot* as "descendants" of the source, he proposed that each *sefira* is capable of regeneration from within – they are like a spiritual genetic code that exists within each person and mirrors a divine code.

A galaxy of scholars lived in the hillside town of Safed.

Cordovero also saw the *sefirot* as vessels that contain and reflect the light of *Ein Sof*. As a practical mystic he attached tremendous importance to including the body in worship and encouraged "the experience of sitting in the presence of divine light". This form of meditation involved closing your eyes and imagining God's light encompassing you.

Breathing and Envisioning the Alphabet

The Hebrew letters are the tools that God used to create the universe.
Meditating on the letters (see page 17) — as the mystics of Safed did —
can allow their energy to enter us as if God were
communicating with us directly.

Stand or sit facing Jerusalem. Straighten your back. Press your upper arms into your body. Extend your forearms, with your hands flat and your palms facing upward. Close your eyes.

Imagine weighing positive force in your right palm and negative force in your left.

Take ten slow, deep breaths, all the way down into your stomach, then back upward and out through your chest.

Picture an image of *Aleph*, the first letter of the Hebrew alphabet. Breathe in gently and allow the letter to move toward you.

Let the letter remain in front of you for a moment. Breathe out slowly as you let the letter recede.

Repeat with each letter of the Hebrew alphabet.

By Abulafia,
based on Sefer Yetzirah 2.1

The Meditation of Avraham, Pupil of Cordovero

God, who is hidden within the beauty of His domain,

Intellect beyond conception,

Highest of all high,

Crowned with the uppermost crown,

We all accept Your Majesty.

From the very beginning of time

Your law was there.

The impact of Your hidden wisdom

Derived from nothing yet from everywhere,

The beginning of wisdom is fear of God.

The rivers of understanding are fountains of faith.

They drip deep into the minds of men,

And out of them come the Five Gates of Intuition.

God creates the Faithful.

Yitschak Luria

Yitschak Luria – known as the *Ari* (Lion), a Hebrew acronym for "the divine Rabbi Isaac" – remains the most popular and influential of all Kabbalists. He wrote little, but his ideas had immense impact.

Yitschak Luria was born in Jerusalem in 1534, but his father died when he was young and he was brought up in Cairo by his uncle Mordechai, a rich scholar. Luria became wealthy in his own right very early in life and devoted himself to study, first the *Talmud* and *halakha* (Jewish law) and then the Kabbalah. At the age of 20, he moved to Safed to study with Moses Cordovero.

Opposite: A silk curtain for a Torah Ark, from a Lurianic community in Istanbul.

After Cordovero died in 1570, Luria inherited Cordovero's mantle and was acknowledged as an innovative thinker and a mystical genius. It was the way he expressed his mysticism through meditation, closeness to nature, song, dance and joy that made him unique (see page 109). He gathered around him many pupils, who became his "missionaries", spreading his ideas throughout the Jewish world. Luria died in 1572 and his grave in Safed remains a place of pilgrimage to this day.

CHAIM VITAL

Luria's favourite pupil and friend was Chaim Vital. He is known as the follower who faithfully rendered Luria's ideas into writing. He saw himself as the guardian of Luria's mystical tradition.

Vital, who was born in Safed in 1542, had also studied with Cordovero. He attached himself to Luria soon after the teacher arrived in Safed, but Vital also became a scholar and rabbinic authority in his own right. In his later life he held rabbinic positions in Jerusalem and Damascus, where he died in 1620.

After Luria's death Vital gathered Luria's 12 principal pupils together, and they agreed that they would accept only Vital's interpretations of Luria as authoritative. He wrote them down in two books: *Etz Chayim* (*The Tree of Life*) and *Etz HaDaat* (*The Tree of Knowledge*). Other writers later challenged him, but Vital remains the supreme source for information on Luria's ideas and practices.

> "When preparing to say the daily prayers … imagine being a pauper before the King's palace. Clothed in the fringed shawl and with tefillin against the heart and against the brain, pronounce the awesome name Adonai, Lord. A lion descends in the angelic form of Michael and takes the words to Heaven."
>
> **ZOHAR I.23B**

Luria's Way of Worship

Luria introduced an ecstatic form of worship that emphasized joy and informality. His mystical theories were revolutionary, and they brought a new passion to religious worship within Judaism.

In the 16th century Judaism was still afflicted by the disastrous loss of its Temple and its homeland. The despondent mood had been deepened by the exiles from Spain and other countries. Like all the Kabbalists, Luria was still committed to the traditional religion but felt that it had lost its excitement and creativity.

He argued that every act – whether part of a religious ritual or an everyday action – should be devoted to God. As all human actions are mirrored on a spiritual level, they have an impact on the soul. It was not enough just to "do the right thing": each person should think and dedicate himself before acting. He composed the following small meditation, which could be recited before any ritual: "Behold I am ready and prepared to perform an act that will unite me with my Creator."

Luria looked for ways in which he could make prayer more meaningful. Despite the traditional avoidance of song – out of mourning for the Temple – he set prayers to music. He was himself a great lyrical poet and several of his songs have entered mainstream liturgy.

Prayer, according to Luria, needed to lose its rigidity. He encouraged his pupils to leave the synagogues, if they felt the spirit move them, and to dance and pray outside in the fields. His message was that we should bring ecstasy back into worship.

Shabbetai Zevi

Kabbalists tried to understand how to bring God's benevolence to Earth. Each catastrophe in Jewish life revived the dream of messianic salvation. But this led to false prophets and disappointed hopes.

By far the most significant false messiah was Shabbetai Zevi, born in Smyrna in 1626. In his early life he was a serious Kabbalist and scholar, but after travelling to Gaza and encountering Nathan Benjamin Levi in 1665, he publicly declared himself the Messiah. Zevi announced that it was time for the Jews to return to Jerusalem.

Zevi veered wildly between periods of despair and ecstasy. During the latter he would openly break Jewish laws and say he had been inspired to do so. This behaviour split communities, and many rabbis opposed him, but he soon won a massive popular following.

In Constantinople in 1666 Zevi was arrested, and given the choice between conversion or death. He converted to Islam, but many followers remained loyal, arguing that he had converted in order to fight evil on its homeground.

Opposite: Zevi attracted followers from around the world who would join him in messianic rituals and ascetic practices.

CHAPTER SIX

LURIANIC KABBALAH

Yitschak Luria was a true spiritual giant, whose impact on Judaism was profound. He was totally committed to Jewish practice as the basis for the Kabbalah, seeing the mystical aspect as a natural extra dimension and refinement of the traditional religion.

Tzimtzum

The theory of *tzimtzum* is one of Luria's most interesting and controversial theories. It is a way of explaining both creation and the origins of good and evil.

Luria did not find contemporary creation theories satisfactory. The orthodox idea that God created the world out of nothing seemed to put too much distance between God and His universe. Earlier mystical theories that God made the world out of Himself did not explain why the world and humanity acted in such an ungodlike way. Luria's alternative was *tzimtzum* (meaning something like "shrinkage" or "contraction").

Until Luria, most mystics had thought that God's first creative act was to send out energy, and this was how He entered the universe. Luria suggested that as the infinite *Ein Sof*, His first act was to "gather in His breath" and, as it were, reduce within Himself. God remained everything He was before, but He now made "space" for the creation of the universe. He then emanated the divine "light" that initiated creation. But as the light was too strong for the material world, He reduced its power by distilling it through the *sefirot* – the intermediaries between *Ein Sof* and the world.

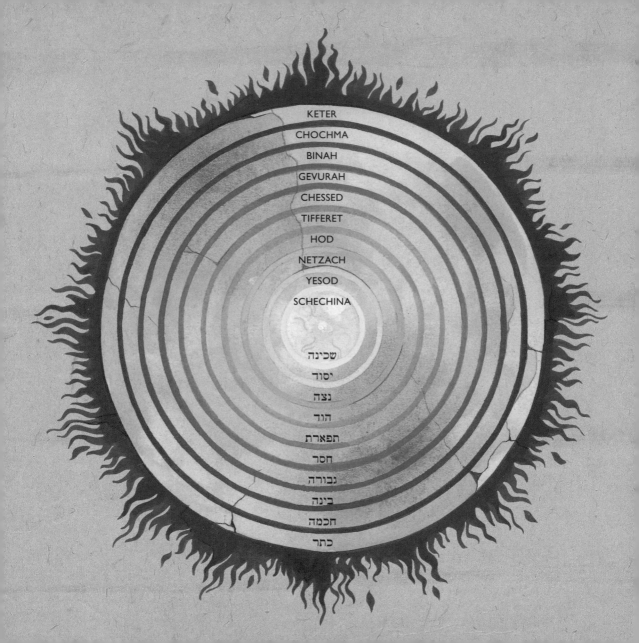

KETER
CHOCHMA
BINAH
GEVURAH
CHESSED
TIFFERET
HOD
NETZACH
YESOD
SCHECHINA

שכינה
יסוד
נצה
הוד
תפארת
חסר
גבורה
בינה
חכמה
כתר

Luria's theory makes the first act of God one of limitation, even withdrawal. But because the emanation stage is rather undefined, different theories later emerged as to what he meant.

According to some Kabbalists, Luria was suggesting that the process of contraction meant that although God still comprised the same qualities, they were somehow dislocated. Out of this "chaos" the quality of *Gevurah* (Power), which is associated with judgment and the proactive right arm of God, emerged as dominant and created the universe. Even mercy was subordinated to *Gevurah*, which is why we sometimes experience the universe as harsh and destructive.

Opposite: The image of the sefirot in concentric spheres was influenced by medieval cosmology, which put Earth at the centre.

Others thought that in the divine space from which God withdrew – called *tehiru* (the purified realm) – *Gevurah* merged with God's energy in the form of light to become the ingredients of the world.

In Vital's explanation of Luria, when God withdrew, a sort of vacuum was created within *Ein Sof*. In this vacuum were formed multidimensional concentric vessels that contained the *sefirot*. *Ein Sof* and the *sefirot* interact: *Ein Sof* "descends" into the *sefirot*, spreading out in a motion called *hitpashtut* that inspires the *sefirot* to form all things; the *sefirot* also move into *Ein Sof* and away from the material world – a process of *histalkut* (withdrawal), which causes negative energy. It is this constant throbbing, in and out, that gives us the feeling that God is active in the world.

The Nature of God

W hen early Kabbalists considered various names of God (see page 64), they were trying to understand and explain the Divine. Luria took this idea onto a deeper level of significance, and tried to define exactly how God relates to His creation.

Mystics in the time of the *Zohar* had devised many new names of God, which related to His different aspects. Luria and his followers expanded on the practice, adding further secret names.

Some of these names are combinations of the letters *Yod*, *Hey*, *Vav*, *Hey*, the principal biblical name of God. Other names comprise all the letters of the Hebrew alphabet in various permutations, as in the ancient kabbalistic poem *Anah Bekoach* (*I plead with You*; see page 121)

or the 231 Gates Meditation (see page 93), which contains 231 possible names, only one of which is "right".

Whereas early scholars used such names as a way of explaining God, Lurianic Kabbalists emphasized that the search for an appropriate divine name was a major part of connecting with Him. We have to consider carefully which of God's energies can help to rectify a particular situation. When we discover the "ineffable" name for this

> "Ein Sof is the soul of the souls of the sefirot, which are the souls of everything …. When Ein Sof generates Atzilut … these souls are distributed throughout the universe. This leads to Beriyah, which leads to Yetzirah until Yetzirah channels Atzilut into Assiyah. All this happens constantly …."
>
> **YESHAYA HOROWITZ (1560–1630), THE HISTORY OF MAN**

aspect, we need to consider it. The name might be written on a charm, or more commonly, added to an existing prayer and meditated on during prayer.

THE FOUR WORLDS

Luria and his followers did not stop with the names of God. They wanted to know not only what God is, but exactly what He *does* – how He works. This they explained in a theory known as the "Four Worlds".

Although the Four World division dates back to the *Sefer Yetzirah*, in Luria it becomes more specifically related to the way in which God relates to the universe. While the ideas of tzimtzum, emanation and the *sefirot* describe the stages of creation, the Four Worlds refer to the different types of divine creativity.

One way to understand these "worlds" is by the analogy of human creativity. First, a man decides or intends to make something. This is the world of

The word Melekh (King) from a Hebrew prayer book. God's name is surrounded by animals as He is involved in all creation.

Atzilut (Emanation). Then he gathers ideas and thinks about it creatively. This is Beriyah (Creation). Next he draws up his plans and gathers the materials. This is the stage of Yetzirah (Formation). Finally, he physically assembles or makes the thing, which is Assiyah (Doing).

Confusingly perhaps, these types of creativity exist simultaneously. Rather than explaining a process, they represent different degrees of divine involvement in the universe. Closest to God is the eternal divine world of Atzilut. Beriyah is the world of mystical knowledge that contains the chariot (see page 32) and archangels. The world of Yetzirah contains the lower angels, men's souls and the forces of the sitra achra (the "other side"). Finally, Assiyah is the material world.

These worlds help to explain how God communicates. Sometimes His intervention in the universe is immediate and direct; at other times His intervention is indirect, and He operates through other vehicles, such as angels. If we can understand the ways in which God sends His energy down to Earth, we can begin to ascend toward the Divine.

The Prayer of Nechunia Ben HaKna

This is a translation of an important kabbalistic prayer, beginning *Anah Bekoach* (I plead with You). The initial letters of each Hebrew word make up a "name" of God. This combination of letters is often used on *shiviti* amulets and prayer sheets.

I plead with You, through the might of Your right,

Untie the physical bonds that restrain us.

Accept the song of Your people,

Raise our souls up and purify us.

Please, Great One, seek out Your faithful ones,

Protect them like Your essence.

Bless them, purify them, give them eternal grace,

Through Your merciful goodness.

Holy Protector, in Your kindness,

Lead your congregation to perfection.

From Luria's Prayer Book

Good and Evil II

The origin of evil and why God allows it to happen is one of the most problematic issues in all religions. The Kabbalah in general, and Luria specifically, have unique ways of explaining why evil exists.

In Luria's scheme there are two different but related parts to good and evil: good and evil in the world in general; and good and evil in mankind.

In the initial act of creation, *Ein Sof* withdrew and into the vacuum placed perfect vessels filled with divine light. But some of these vessels could not survive the withdrawal of *Ein Sof* and they

Opposite: The letter Mem (right) represents good, Shin (left) evil. Aleph is the fulcrum around which these balance.

smashed. The three upper *sefirot* – sometimes associated with intellect or soul – retained the light, but the more physical lower seven could not.

This is Luria's theory of *shevirat keilim* (smashing the vessels). The cataclysm caused the release of two substances: divine light, the source of all good in the world; and *klippot* (shards or shells). Although creation was still possible using a combination of the two substances, the incomplete and imperfect *klippot* are the source of evil in the world.

A crown used to decorate the Torah. Obedience to the Torah is a way to return to the purity of creation.

In a sense we could say that the world we experience was not how God originally intended it, and therefore that evil exists as an accident. But another explanation is that God meant to give our souls the opportunity to struggle to correct or rectify the shattered system.

This leads to the second aspect of good and evil: that of human actions. The function of the soul is to try to reconcile and rebuild the broken pieces. These shards are not evil in themselves, they are just incomplete. Similarly, we, who are made of the *klippot* and divine light, are not intrinsically evil: we are simply imperfect. This is why, like Adam and Eve, we sometimes simply make the wrong choices.

To become fuller people we need to join with the Divine. This involves using all the *sefirot* and the whole body to follow the *Torah*. Everyone has the capacity to "correct" him- or herself, and if enough souls purify themselves, then we can perfect the universe.

Preparation for Morning Prayer

This *kavvanah* (see page 80) highlights the importance of the *talit* (a prayer shawl with fringed corners). The shawl creates a protective aura of spirituality around the body.

Behold I am ready and prepared.

I dedicate myself to Your holy name, blessed be it,

And to Your divine presence.

As I tremble before You I beg Your mercy,

And begging Your mercy I wish to declare the divine unity

That is represented by the letters *Yod Hey* together with *Vav Hey*.

This is the complete unity of God as it applies to all His people.

And with this I cover my body in the shawl and fringes.

So all my 248 limbs and 365 sinews are clothed in the divine spirit which descends through Your 613 commandments.

And just as I cover myself in this world, so may I achieve the holy covering from You, the garment of scholarship and study,

In the world to come, in the Garden of Eden.

And may this act of covering protect me, my being, my soul and my spirit from all external forces. May it protect me as an eagle spreads its wings over its young.

From Luria's Prayer Book

Adam Kadmon

The term *Adam Kadmon* literally means "primordial Man", and early Kabbalists used it to describe the first human God created in the Garden of Eden. But Luria extended the meaning to include the original matter out of which humanity was created.

Luria developed a specific idea of *Adam Kadmon*, which became a source of much controversy. He suggested that after *Ein Sof* withdrew in the process of *tzimtzum*, the first stage of emanation led to the emergence of a sort of refined matter called *Adam Kadmon*. This was not only the original human, but was the material out of which all creation was formed. In the Four Worlds theory (see page 119), *Adam Kadmon* was the material gathered together during *Yetzirah* (Formation).

In this tradition *Adam Kadmon* is often depicted as a circle encompassing other circles. This symbolizes the presence of the *sefirot* in the physical world. Everything is suffused with God's various energies. In some versions *Adam Kadmon* is drawn as a circle, like an ovum, which slowly transforms into a figure. This is different from earlier kabbalistic ideas that had applied the *sefirot* to specific parts of a human outline. Man did not spring into existence as a fully

The Golem

Out of the idea of *Adam Kadmon* emerged the concept of the Golem. The word *golem* actually means "matter" and was commonly used by Hebrew philosophers to describe the lowest level of human existence. In the *Bible*, when Adam was first fashioned out of the dust of the Earth, this was the Golem. God breathed the *neshama* (breath of life) into him, and he became "a living being".

Some Kabbalists dabbled in the fantasy of creating life, a "Superman" who would guard the Jewish community. As the word *neshama* included the word *shem* (name), it was thought that placing the correct name of God in an effigy might bring it to life.

formed human, but developed in a more organic way, incorporating God's energies throughout the entire body.

Luria also associated levels of the soul with this circular *Adam Kadmon*. The Zohar had explained the different types of soul (see page 72), ranging from the *nefesh* (lifeforce) which animates all living things, through the *ruach* (spirit) and *neshama* (breath of life), right up to the *ot* (living essence), which is beyond words, and the *yechida* (unity), which is closest to the divine origins. Just as the *sefirot* permeate *Adam Kadmon*, so, too, does *Adam Kadmon* contain all souls, with *ot* and *yechida* closest to the core.

Tikkun

The word *tikkun* means "to rectify". It describes how we can try to achieve spiritual perfection both in ourselves and in the wider material world. This is achieved by living a spiritual way of life, getting as close to God as possible through kabbalistic practice.

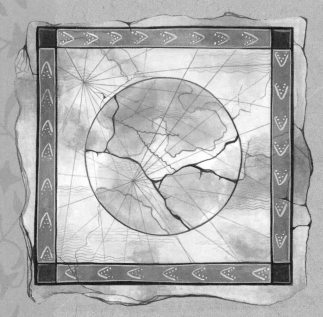

The idea of tikkun had existed before Luria, but he turned it into the positive goal of spirituality. Relating it to his creation theories, he suggested that we should all actively seek the divine light and look for ways of rectifying the *klippot*, to reconstruct the world in the perfect form originally intended.

Each of us needs to live a holy life in order to accomplish tikkun, the re-creation of the world as a perfect whole.

> "There are three ways of repairing that which has been divided and separated from God. The first is the repair of the self. The second is the repair of the world. And the third is the repair of the divine presence. All were united in the divine Ein Sof before the cataclysm of creation produced chaos."
>
> **YESHAYA HOROWITZ (1560–1630), TWO TABLETS OF THE COVENANT**

As a direct emanation from God, divine light can give us the spiritual ability to correct the world. Finding it requires us to abide by the *Torah* and to use mystical practices such as *devekut* (see page 43), *kavvanot* (see page 80) and meditation. At the same time, we must also overcome the obstacles of life that arise out of the *klippot*.

However, it is not enough simply to go through the motions. The process of *tikkun* cannot succeed without our constantly thinking about each different aspect of the *sefirot* as they are within ourselves and within God. The *sefirot* should be involved in all our actions and thoughts, not just the religious ones. We should always be asking ourselves: am I thinking with both *Binah* and *Chochma*, or am I acting with both *Gevurah* and *Chessed*? Every part of our being has to be involved in this process of "reconciliation", and this must be true of everyone for *tikkun* to succeed.

Purity

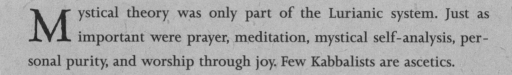

Mystical theory was only part of the Lurianic system. Just as important were prayer, meditation, mystical self-analysis, personal purity, and worship through joy. Few Kabbalists are ascetics.

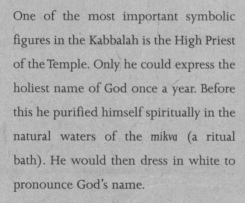

One of the most important symbolic figures in the Kabbalah is the High Priest of the Temple. Only he could express the holiest name of God once a year. Before this he purified himself spiritually in the natural waters of the *mikva* (a ritual bath). He would then dress in white to pronounce God's name.

Luria borrowed these motifs and applied them to his system. It was – and is – a Jewish custom to wash before prayers, but Luria suggested that the *mikva* should be used at the start of each day to dedicate the body to God's service. Luria and his followers also wore simple white shifts, white skull-caps and shawls around their heads to remind themselves of the need to maintain their level of purity throughout the day.

Followers of Luria prepared for prayers by bowing and prostrating themselves, in imitation of rituals that were used in the Temple. Part of their services would involve walking toward Jerusalem at sunset singing psalms. The group would then split, some of them returning to the synagogue and some remaining in the hills.

It was Luria who instituted *Kabbalat Shabbat* (Receiving the Sabbath), which is still practised in many synagogues today. This preparation for the Friday night service includes the mystical poem *Lekhah Dodi* (*Come, My Beloved*), which is followed by bowing toward the sunset. *Kabbalat Shabbat* was intended as a way of making the day more meaningful and personal. The Sabbath is welcomed as the Bride of Israel, a day on which God's glory is apparent in the *Schechina*, the feminine Presence of God.

Luria also stressed the importance of pleasure, by extending meals, especially Sabbath and festive ones. He argued that unless we enjoy a legitimate pleasure we are rejecting a divine gift.

"Purity is the way to improve the heart and the mind. As we find in Psalms, 'God has created a pure heart.' And the purpose of purity is to ensure that a person leaves no space within, nor any opportunity without, for the evil inclination. All actions should be based on wisdom and respect for God rather than on desire and evil. This applies equally to the material world as it does to the spiritual."

MOSES CHAIM LUZZATTO (1707–46), THE PATHS OF THE JUST

Meditation on Purity

Before eating or praying, we must purify ourselves.

This is how to purify the hands. As you approach the water you say:

I am ready and prepared to purify myself in Your holy name so that I may fulfil Your will in purity and perfection.

The right hand I raise to Mother and my five fingers are Her five *sefirot*; they point up to Heaven but they are weighed down by impurity. I lower them, and with my left hand I raise the cup and pour a quarter-measure of pure water from my wrist down to my fingers.

I take up the cup with my right hand. I raise my left to Father with His five *sefirot*. I lower them to remove their impurity, and with my right hand I raise the cup and pour water over the left hand from my wrist to the fingers.

Before I eat I must wash each hand three times. But this holiness is a higher holiness than the priests in the holy Temple – may it be rebuilt in our days – were required to undertake before eating their tithes.

Chaim Vital, from Hanhagot HaAri

ויהי בימי אחשורוש
הוא אחשורוש המלך מהדו
ועד כוש שבע ועשרים ומאה מדינה
בימים ההם כשבת המלך אחשורוש
על כסא מלכותו אשר בשושן הבירה
בשנת שלוש למלכו עשה משתה
לכל שריו ועבדיו חיל פרס ומדי
הפרתמים ושרי המדינות לפניו בהראתו
את עשר כבוד מלכותו ואת יקר תפארת
גדולתו ימים רבים שמונים ומאת
יום ובמלואת הימים האלה עשה המלך לכל העם
הנמצאים בשושן הבירה למגדול ועד קטן משתה
שבעת ימים בחצר גנת ביתן המלך
חור כרפס ותכלת אחוז בחבלי בוץ וארגמן
על גלילי כסף ועמודי שש מטות זהב וכסף
על רצפת בהט ושש ודר וסחרת והשקות
בכלי זהב וכלים מכלים שונים ויין
מלכות רב כיד המלך והשתיה כדת אין אנס
כי כן יסד המלך על כל רב ביתו לעשות
כרצון איש ואיש
גם ושתי המלכה
עשתה משתה נשים בית המלכות אשר למלך

CHAPTER SEVEN

HASIDISM AND THE KABBALAH TODAY

After false messiahs like Shabbetai Zevi,
the Kabbalah slowly fell out of favour in the
"Enlightened" West. In Eastern Europe, however,
the Kabbalah came to be associated almost
exclusively with Hasidism. In the Middle East
mysticism came to be associated with a few
masters known as *mekubbalim*.

After Luria and Hasidism

L uria's revival of ecstatic mysticism led directly to Hasidism – a movement founded in 18th-century Eastern Europe. Hasidism is probably the most important mystical element in Judaism today.

Yitschak Luria died in 1572, but the Kabbalah continued to win followers. One factor that contributed to its growth was the development of printing. Seventeenth-century texts such as *Shenei Luchot HaBrit* (*Two Tablets of the Covenant*), by Rabbi Yeshaya Horowitz, are still essential reading in orthodox academies.

Although Shabbetai Zevi was a false prophet, by the mid-17th century he had helped to popularize the Kabbalah. In contrast, one of the most influential Middle Eastern Kabbalists after Luria

wanted to withdraw mysticism from the public domain. Shalom Sharabi of Yemen (1720–77) thought that the Kabbalah should be an exclusive esoteric study, and to this end he founded the academy of Beth El in Jerusalem. This became the training ground for many important Kabbalists until it was destroyed by an earthquake in 1927.

In Eastern Europe the Kabbalah took a very different direction when the popular movement of Hasidism was founded by a figure called the Baal Shem Tov.

THE BAAL SHEM TOV

Israel Ben Eliezer was born around 1698 in Podolia (now in Ukraine). As a young man he lived in poverty, but at the age of 36 he revealed himself to be a *Baal Shem Tov*. Literally meaning "Having the Good Name", this was a person who could use divine names to cure or help the poor.

The Baal Shem Tov set off around the Jewish settlements of Eastern Europe

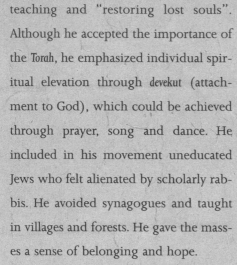

teaching and "restoring lost souls". Although he accepted the importance of the *Torah*, he emphasized individual spiritual elevation through *devekut* (attachment to God), which could be achieved through prayer, song and dance. He included in his movement uneducated Jews who felt alienated by scholarly rabbis. He avoided synagogues and taught in villages and forests. He gave the masses a sense of belonging and hope.

His movement caught on quickly but aroused the opposition of the established rabbinate, who feared that the teachings of the *Torah* would be watered down and that Judaism would suffer the abuses of previous mass movements. Eastern European Jewry soon split into rival camps: the *Hasidim*, who took their name from the *Hasidei Ashkenaz* (see page 42); and the *Mitnagdim* (the opponents).

THE GROWTH OF HASIDISM

The Baal Shem Tov died in 1760, but his successors were exceptional mystical leaders in their own right. The first of them, Dov Baer of Mezerich and Yakov Yosef of Polonoye, were innovative and charismatic. They established "courts", where followers could gather and learn from their teachers. Emissaries were sent out all over Eastern Europe and the Middle East to spread the ideology. New groups emerged that revolved around the personality of their leaders (see box opposite). In time these leaders were able to establish their own dynasties.

For all their differences, the separate hasidic branches shared ideas of informal worship, dedication to God in all thoughts and actions, and special dress — long black coats, fur hats and beards. This not only helped social cohesion,

The Tzaddik

Hasidic leaders were called *rebbes*, to distinguish them from the more academic rabbis. The *rebbe* was seen as a *tzaddik*, a saintly man who, through his personality and devotion, had the task of inspiring every member of his flock. People would spend Sabbaths and festivals at the *rebbe's* court, praying, singing, eating and drinking.

Although the *rebbe* was never supposed to be an intermediary between man and God, inevitably many Hasidim tended to treat him as such. The custom developed of giving him *kvitelech*, written requests for blessings – for a family member, money or health. Some would donate money to the *rebbe* or even make him a business partner.

but also reinforced their sense of being dedicated to a spiritual and mystical way of life.

In recent years, despite the decimation of the Holocaust, Hasidism has revived to the point where it now dominates the orthodox world. Despite being ideologically restrictive, it is still mystically creative. The most public of its sects is Lubavitch–Chabad, which originated in Russia but is now based in New York. The sect is dynamic in its outreach and use of modern marketing techniques to spread its message. At root it is highly messianic and uses liberal and ecstatic forms of worship.

Joy, Dance and Music

From the start, Hasidism combined the holistic and ecstatic aspects of the Kabbalah. Every part of us – mind, body and spirit – must be devoted to worship.

Hasidism was inspired by *Psalm* 100: "Serve God through joy and through song." *Simcha* (joy) became its motto. The idea was to defeat sin and temptation by positively striving for joy rather than negatively avoiding temptation. Another important term was *hitla'avut* (enthusiasm). Every religious act had to be undertaken with *hitla'avut*.

Song and music played a crucial role in hasidic worship. Singing accompanied formal services, and each dynasty composed tunes that drew on local non-Jewish traditions and gave a specific flavour to its services. Hasidic music today shows clear Russian, Polish, Hungarian and Turkish influences. This was justified ideologically by the idea that the divine light of sincere worship would eradicate any imperfect "dross" that might have entered a song from "profane" origins. In this sense music not only purified the soul but the soul could also purify music.

Equally important to Hasidism are the *nigunim* (songs without words). Some are

lively and used for dancing, others are slow and reflective and are used to aid meditation and devotion. *Nigunim* and other instrumental pieces play an important part in wedding celebrations and weekday gatherings. During the times of the hasidic courts, such events were also occasions for performances by *badchanim* (jokers and court jesters).

A detail of musicians taken from a 14th-century Passover service.

There are three main types of hasidic dance: the slow, dignified solo of the *rebbe* or other important figure; the wild, *hora*-like circles of young men; and the mass dances in procession. Women's dances were separate but equally lively.

Hasidic Prayer

It was in prayer that Hasidism showed its strongest links to the classical Kabbalah: prayer was a way of transcending the mundane. It was not an occasion to ask things of God, but a way of transporting humans to a higher level.

The Baal Shem Tov believed that prayer was a means of "warming the universe", a way of bringing the divine light to mankind. This light would bring both hope and "enlightenment". The challenge of prayer was to overcome negative or evil thoughts that came from the "other side" of the *sefirot* and transform them into positive ones.

The initial vehicle of prayer is the *dibbur* (spoken word), but as a person prays he or she must move beyond words, until they are praying in the realm of *machshava* (thought). To help worshippers to transcend the text, hasidic prayer is often rapid. Another technique for rising above the words is to visualize the Hebrew letters of the text. These have a spiritual form of their own, which can direct our thought toward God. The letters recede as we begin to engage with the Divine.

In many ways hasidic prayer is intense, but in other ways it is relaxed.

A prayer book of the hasidic
Lubavitch–Chabad movement.

While it is more traditional to pray standing still in a state of awe before God, hasidic prayer is lively, filled with songs and rhythms. It is accompanied by *shockelling* (shaking the body) as a way of involving all the limbs, whipping up enthusiasm and achieving ecstasy. This *avodah gashmi* (physical act of worship) should parallel the *avodah ruchani* (spiritual act of worship).

Hasidic prayer also has a certain optimism and familiarity about it. It is usual to stop in the middle of a prayer and improvise a personal conversation with God. You pray with the conviction that you are talking to a friend rather than a remote being.

The Prayer of Rabbi Elimelech

Elimelech of Liszensk was an 18th-century *rebbe* who believed that he could help to raise the spiritual level of his followers. He was known for his prayers and supplications.

May it be Your will, *YHVH*, our God and God of our fathers,

That you should listen to the sincere cries of Your people

And give ear to the prayers of Your faithful with mercy.

Prepare our hearts and correct our thoughts and let our prayers flow easily to You.

Bend Your ear to listen to the pleas of Your servants who appeal to Your mercy with broken cries and shattered spirits.

You know full well how weak we are and how difficult it is for us to reach up to You and to attach ourselves to Your divine spirit.

Help us to drive away distractions.

Prevent any evil thoughts from intervening between us and You.

May our thoughts be pure and clear before You that we may believe with complete faith in your divinity, unity and benevolence.

Meditation before each Sabbath Meal

Luria suggested that meals should be religious occasions,
especially on Sabbaths and festivals. Food could be combined with divine service,
by listening to the *Torah* and singing songs.

I am preparing this special meal
That is dedicated to the source of all complete and true belief
And I delight in the presence of the Holy King.
I am preparing the meal of the King.
This is the meal of the Lesser Face of God.
The ancient Holy One invites us to eat of the holy food
brought to this meal with Him.

By Yitschak Luria

Mystical Alternatives,
Then and Now

While Hasidism flourished, the Kabbalah took other directions elsewhere. Its ideas also spread into other religions. Today the Kabbalah is experiencing a surge of new interest – from Jews and non-Jews alike – but the authenticity of some sects should be questioned.

WONDER MYSTICS

In the 17th century the town of Safed lost much of its textile industry, and many Jews left. The mystical tradition polarized. While Hasidism flourished in Eastern Europe, different forms took root in the oriental Jewish communities – Yemen, Syria and the Mediterranean countries of north-west Africa. Here there were no significant sects or large-scale movements, but mysticism became an important part of most communities. The mainstream rabbinate often used the Kabbalah as a means of exercising control as well as giving support and reassurance to the poor through kabbalistic charms and blessings.

Individual masters, or *mekubbalim*, were also revered. Some were genuine practical Kabbalists. In fact, most of today's true Kabbalists practising in Israel come from these communities.

However, a few mystics in these areas laid claim to being "wonder rabbis". These figures would possess "skills" ranging from palm- and skull-reading to the ability to tell fortunes with astrology or by "reading" religious artefacts.

CHRISTIAN KABBALAH

The Zohar attracted the attention of Christian theologians as far back as the 15th century. Since then some popes have seen the Kabbalah as dangerous and subversive, while others have welcomed its contribution to Christian beliefs.

The first significant Christian to take an interest in the Kabbalah was Giovanni

A stained-glass window at the Central National Library, Israel, showing the sefirot in the shape of the Tree of Life.

Pico Della Mirandola (1463–94) of Florence. He studied the *Zohar* with Spanish Jews and lectured on the Kabbalah in Rome in 1486. He argued that its ideas on the *sefirot* as the way in which God interacts with mankind offered support for the Christian Trinity.

Mirandola influenced Johannes Reuchlin, the German Hebraist and theologian who wrote *On the Science of Kabbalah* in 1517. Reuchlin used the kabbalistic idea that God manifests Himself through different names to argue that each divine revelation was building up to the appearance of God as *Shaddai* (Jesus). These scholars inspired, in turn, the French thinker Guillaume Postel, who translated the *Sefer Yetzirah* and the *Zohar* into Latin, and the Austrian Johann Albrecht Widdmanstetter, who built up a library of books on the Kabbalah and researched the movement's influence on Islamic mysticism. In 1684 Knorr Von Rosenroth's *Kabbalah Denudata* was the first book to explain the Kabbalah to a general non-Jewish audience.

But despite this interest and the shared religious roots, the Kabbalah never took hold in Christianity in the same way as it did in Judaism, and it has become very much a minority interest.

THE KABBALAH TODAY

Jewish mysticism has always contained a strong element of messianism – the idea that a saviour will bring peace and a return to Israel. But the Jewish people did not have the means or confidence to declare a state of Israel until 1948. This return reinvigorated the messianic impetus and led to an increase in the number of Kabbalah study centres.

Israel was also the home of the German-born academic Gershom Scholem (1897–1982). In the 20th century he has helped perhaps more than any other to reestablish serious study of the Kabbalah. Unfortunately, in today's world a gap has opened up between academic theory and the actual practice of living a mystical life.

Another recent phenomenon is the emergence of many new groups in the West that teach a watered-down version of the Kabbalah. As the world becomes technologically more sophisticated, many people look to earlier ways of understanding life. Whereas many Western religions can seem dry, routine and unattractive, charismatic mysticism has become a popular alternative.

However, to be authentic, kabbalistic teaching needs to be deeply rooted in Jewish religious practice. If it is removed or detached, it becomes trivial and superficial. You cannot "buy" spirituality in the form of candles, water or red bands. A genuine experience of the Kabbalah is available today only in a few centres in Safed and Jerusalem. Even then it is open only to those who have studied and who practise a spiritual life.

But for the majority of us who cannot access this experience, there is still much that we can learn from the Kabbalah. Its mystical insights can help us to understand and improve the human situation. In its holistic approach the Kabbalah explains how all aspects of our lives interact – physical, mental, emotional and spiritual. If we are aware of these aspects and focus on balancing them, we can hope to elevate our lives, as well as those of the people around us.

Table of Important Dates

The following is a list of historical periods, events, figures and texts mentioned in this book. For ease of reference, dates are given in the Gregorian rather than the Jewish calendar. Titles of texts are in italics.

c.1900–1600 BCE	Patriarchal period
c.1250–1230 BCE	Exodus from Egypt
1084–1014 BCE	King David
9th century BCE	*Elijah*
8th century BCE	*Isaiah*
722 BCE	Northern Kingdom (Israel) destroyed
586 BCE	Jerusalem and First Temple destroyed
6th century BCE	*Ezekiel*
586–538 BCE	Babylonian exile
538 BCE	First return to Israel
c.520–c.515 BCE	Building of Second Temple
c.5th century BCE	*Daniel*
356–323 BCE	Alexander the Great
333–63 BCE	Hellenistic period
168–37 BCE	Maccabean rule; Qumran community established near Dead Sea
c.37 BCE–4 CE	Herod's rule
70 CE	Jerusalem and Second Temple destroyed
1st century	Shimon Ben Yochai and Nechunia Ben HaKna
c.135–c.220	Judah the Prince
c.200	*Mishnah* compiled
c.200–1300	*Hekhalot* literature
c.200–c.600	The *Sefer Yetzirah* (Book of Creation)

c.300	Jerusalem *Talmud* compiled
c.6th century	Babylon *Talmud* compiled
8th–9th centuries	Jewish migrations into northern Europe and Spain
1040–1105	Rabbi Shlomo Yitzchaki (Rashi)
1095–1291	Crusades
c.12th century	The *Bahir* (*Book of Light*)
12th–13th centuries	*Hasidei Ashkenaz*
1135–1204	Maimonides
c.1160–1236	Isaac the Blind
1182	Expulsion of Jews from France
1194–1270	Nachmanides
1240–c.1291	Abraham Abulafia
1248–c.1325	Josef Gikatilla
c.1250–1305	Moses de León
c.1290	The *Zohar* (*Brightness*)
1488–1575	Joseph Caro
1492	Expulsion of Jews from Spain
1500	Increased settlement in Safed
1522–70	Moses Cordovero
1525–1609	Judah Loew, the Maharal of Prague
1534–72	Yitschak Luria
c.1542–1620	Chaim Vital
1560–1630	Yeshaya Horowitz (Shelah)
1626–76	Shabbatei Zevi
c.1698–1760	Baal Shem Tov
1707–46	Moses Chaim Luzzatto
18th century	Mystics of Beth El
1897–1982	Gershom Scholem
1948	State of Israel founded

Glossary

Adam Kadmon primordial Man; in Lurianic theory the original matter of all creation

Baal Shem Tov a mystic who can use the names of God to change the world; specifically, the founder of Hasidism

Bahir (Book of Light) important mystical text; appeared in 12th-century Provence, attributed to Rabbi Nechunia Ben HaKna

Binah the *sefira* of Understanding

Chessed the *sefira* of Kindness or Love, also called *Gedulla*

Chochma the *sefira* of Wisdom

devekut literally "attachment"; the mystic idea that we can merge with God

double letters Hebrew letters that have a hard or soft sound depending on context; they represent ambiguity in mysticism

Ein Sof the infinite, nonmaterial God that existed before the process of creation

Elohim the first name of God mentioned in the *Bible*; literally means "judges"

End of Days the idea that the world will end and a new order of peace emerge

Gemara part of the *Talmud*; comprises laws, ideas and customs based on the *Mishnah*

Gevurah the *sefira* of Power, also called *Din* (Judgment)

Haggadah scripture telling the story of exodus from Egypt, read at Passover

halakha all Jewish laws and customs

Hasidei Ashkenaz literally "Pious Men of Germany", an ascetic movement that emerged in 12th–13th century Europe

Hasidism kabbalistic movement founded in 18th-century Eastern Europe by Baal Shem Tov; emphasized individual spiritual elevation through ecstatic worship; now a dominant force in orthodox Judaism

hekhalot literature writing that sought to understand the "heavenly halls"

Hod the *sefira* of Splendour

kabbalah Hebrew term meaning "to receive" or "tradition"

Kabbalah, the body of mystical Jewish literature that emerged in medieval Spain and France

kavvanot exercises that help a mystic to focus on prayer and feel close to God

kemeya an amulet, often decorated with names of God to harness divine energy

Keter the *sefira* of the Crown, also called *Ayin* (Nothingness)

klippot the broken shards or shells left over from the process of creation; the source of evil in the world

ma'aseh bereishit talmudic theme explaining the "secrets of creation"

ma'aseh mercava talmudic theme explaining the "secrets of the chariot"; relates to Ezekiel's vision and mysticism in general

Messiah God's messenger to save mankind; often associated with Elijah or a descendant of King David

Midrash rabbinic method of using biblical texts to explain and teach Jewish ideas

mikva a ritual bath, originally used by priests to prepare for serving in the Temple, later used more widely

Mishnah the part of the *Talmud* that records "Oral Law" established in the first 1,000 years after the *Bible*

mother letters the Hebrew letters *Aleph, Mem* and *Shin*; said to represent the elements of creation – air, water and fire

Netzach the *sefira* of Endurance

partzufim literally "faces"; the male and female aspects of primordial Man, which mirror the Faces of God

Pentateuch the first five books of the *Bible*, also referred to as the *Torah*

Sabbath the seventh day of the week, when humanity is closest to God

Sabbath Bride or Queen idea that the Sabbath represents the union of the physical world with the spiritual

Schechina the *sefira* of God's Presence, also known as *Malchut* (Kingdom)

Sefer Yetzirah (*Book of Creation*) appeared after 200 CE; first mystical book to describe the *sefirot* in detail

sefirot (sing. sefira) the ten divine categories or energies through which *Ein Sof* created the universe and communicates with humanity; they are mirrored in humans and reflect the ways in which we function and experience God

shiur koma literature texts concerned with understanding the nature of Man as a way of getting closer to God

shiviti type of plaque decorated with divine names and phrases from the *Psalms*, used as a focus during prayer

single letters Hebrew letters that have one sound; seen by Kabbalists as the stable building blocks of creation

sitra achra the "other side", the negative aspects of the *sefirot*

talit a shawl with four fringed corners, worn during prayer to symbolize divine envelopment of the material world

Talmud very important Jewish text comprising the *Mishnah* and the *Gemara*

tefillin small boxes holding biblical passages, strapped to the arm and head to "bind" a person to God during prayer

Temple, the built by Solomon in the tenth century BCE to house the Ark of the Covenant; destroyed in 586 BCE.

A Second Temple was built c.520 BCE, but destroyed by the Romans in 70 CE

Tifferet the *sefira* of Beauty, also called *Rachamim* (Compassion)

tikkun literally "to rectify"; in Lurianic Kabbalah relates to repair of the divine vessels broken during creation

Torah the first five books of the *Bible* and the revelation given to Moses; generally, the ethical and ritual laws of Judaism

Tree of Life one of the two trees in the Garden of Eden; represents how God interacts with the world

tzimtzum Lurianic theory that *Ein Sof* withdrew inside Himself to make space for creation

Yesod the *sefira* of Foundation

YHVH the "essential" name of God, pronounced only once a year by the High Priest of the Temple; referred to as *Hashem* (The Name)

Zohar (*Brightness*) mystical commentary on the *Torah*, and the most important kabbalistic book; appeared in 14th-century Spain, attributed to Shimon Ben Yochai

Further Reading

Academic History and Analysis

Encyclopedia Judaica. Philadephia, PA: Coronet
Books Inc., 1994.

Green, Arthur. Tormented Master: The Life and Spiritual
Quest of Rabbi Nahman of Bratslav. Woodstock, VT:
Jewish Lights, 1992.

Idel, Moshe. Absorbing Perfections: Kabbalah and
Interpretation. New Haven, CT, and London:
Yale University Press, 2002.

Idel, Moshe. Messianic Mystics. New Haven, CT,
and London: Yale University Press, 2000.

Idel, Moshe. The Mystical Experience in Abraham
Abulafia. Albany, NY, and London: State
University of New York Press, 1988.

Idel, Moshe. Studies in Ecstatic Kabbalah. Albany,
NY, and London: State University of New
York Press, 1988.

Kaplan, Aryeh. Chasidic Masters: History, Biography,
Thought. Jerusalem: Moznaim Publishing
Corp., 1991.

Kaplan, Aryeh. Jewish Meditation. A Practical Guide.
New York: Schoken, 1995.

Kaplan, Aryeh. Meditation and Kabbalah. York Beach,
ME, and London: Red Wheel/Weiser, 1986.

Scholem, Gershom. Major Trends in Jewish
Mysticism. New York: Schoken, 1995.

Scholem, Gershom. On The Kabbalah and its
Symbolism. New York: Schoken, 1996.

Primary Texts

Cordovero, Moses. The Palm Tree of Deborah.
New York: Judaica, 1981.

Gikatilla, Joseph. Gates of Light. Lanham, MD:
Altamira, 1998.

Kaplan, Aryeh, trans. Bahir. York Beach,
ME, and London: Red Wheel/
Weiser, 1990.

Kaplan, Aryeh ed. Sefer Yetzirah. York Beach,
ME, and London: Red Wheel/
Weiser, 1997.

Luria, Isaac and Vital, Chaim. Shaar HaGilgulim:
The Gates of Reincarnation. Thirty Seven Books
Publishing, 2003.

Matt, Daniel C., trans. The Zohar: Pritzker Edition.
Palo Alto, CA: Stanford University Press,
2003.

Simon, Maurice, trans. Zohar. New York:
Soncino Press Ltd, 1934.

Index

Acknowledgments

The publisher would like to thank the following people, museums and photographic libraries for permission to reproduce their material. Every care has been taken to trace copyright holders. However, if we have omitted anyone we apologize and will, if informed, make corrections to any future edition.

Key:
AKG   AKG-images, London
BAL   Bridgeman Art Library, London
BL   British Library, London
Haas   Getty/Stone/Ernst Haas

11 Photolibrary.com/Nathan Bilow; 18 Corbis/Nathan Benn; 20 BAL/BL; 23 AKG/BL; 29 Haas; 32 AKG/Biblioteca Nacional, Madrid; 34 Corbis/Macduff Everton; 39 Haas; 47 Biblioteca Nacional, Lisbon (Ms. Il 72, f.448v); 48 BL; 51 AKG/BL; 55 BL; 56 Haas; 59 AKG/Erich Lessing; 73 Haas; 76 Heritage Image Partnership/BL; 79 BL; 81 Haas; 84 BL; 89 Jewish Museum, London; 90 Corbis/Archivo Iconografico, S.A./Bibliothèque Nationale, Paris; 96 AKG/BL; 97 AKG/Biblioteca Nacional, Madrid; 100 Getty/Stone/Tom Till; 106 Scala/Jewish Museum, New York/The H. Ephraim and Mordecai Benguiat family collection, S4; 112 Photolibrary.com/Jon Arnold; 115 Haas; 120 Art Archive/The Bodleian Library, Oxford (Arch Selden A 6 folio 1v); 124 Corbis/Elio Ciol; 132 Eyewire; 134 AKG/Judaica-Collection Max Berger/Erich Lessing; 137 Getty/Stone/Joerg Hardtke; 141 BL; 143 Magnum Photos, London/Abbas; 147 ©Mordechai Ardon/National Library at the Hebrew University, Jerusalem. photo: Art Directors/Ark Religion/Itzhak Genut

Author's acknowledgments:

I would like to acknowledge the Nazir, from whom I first learned about the Kabbalah; and I would like to thank my editor, Kirsten, and my wife and children.